new salads

starters • classics • mains • sides • dressings

THE AUSTRALIAN
Women's Weekly

When we started this book, we knew we wanted to include our take on the classics, like caesar and niçoise, but we also felt we wanted to give you some really different choices: salads that could rise handsomely to an occasion, or be eaten with a fork from a bowl in front of the TV. We hope our final selection will appeal to everyone who wants to eat more healthily as much as it does to those passionate about cooking.

Pamela Clark

Food Director

contents

introduction	4
starters	6
classics	34
mains	48
sides	88
dressings	110
glossary	114
conversion chart	117
index	118

SALADS ARE FAR MORE THAN JUST TEMPTATION FOR THE TASTEBUDS: THEY'RE ALSO PART OF A RECIPE FOR GOOD HEALTH

It's only been during the recent past that we've seen the salad gain street cred in the culinary world. Before that, it was more or less something of an afterthought: the toss of a few green leaves in a bowl with a slice each of onion and tomato, drowned in bottled dressing, served alongside the main course. Now, however, the increased availability of so many lettuce varieties and the discovery of previously unfamiliar Asian and Mediterranean herbs and vegetables means there's nothing boring about salad ingredients. Plus, contemporary concerns with health and diet as well as lifestyle demands for faster and easier one-dish meals have made the idea of a salad as the focal point of a meal jump to the top of the charts. More and more frequently seen on restaurant menus and just as popular as a dining-in choice, salads make a perfect evening main course. They are relatively easy and quick to prepare; they provide a controlled intake of carbs and fats before bedtime; they are perfect for temperate winters and hot summers; and as delicious as they are nutritious. Salads provide an easy way to make sure you eat five or more different-coloured and types of fruits and vegetables every day as part of a plan for a healthier life. These will give you a wide range of vitamins and minerals that help maintain good health, increase energy levels, protect against the effects of ageing, and even reduce the risk of getting some diseases. Locally grown fruits and vegetables are abundant and enormous in range, and most are available year-round. Balancing their flavours and textures is an exciting and creative way to cook, and imagination can easily take over if you're short of time or one particular ingredient: you can't get it wrong or risk a failure when you're making a salad.

A SALAD AS A STARTER IS ALWAYS A SMART CHOICE FOR A MEAL WHEN THE MAIN COURSE IS RICH AND QUITE SUBSTANTIAL

Pecorino, the Italian word used to describe generic sheep-milk cheese, is generally specifically named after the region in which it was produced: Romano from Rome, Sardo from Sardinia, Siciliano from Sicily and Toscano from Tuscany. A spicy variation of this cheese is pepato, where whole black peppercorns are added to the cheese when it's being made, before ageing; using pepato in this salad would add just a complementary note of piquancy.

asparagus and spinach
with poached egg and pecorino

PREPARATION TIME 10 MINUTES
COOKING TIME 5 MINUTES **SERVES** 4

340g asparagus, trimmed
4 eggs
200g baby spinach leaves, trimmed
1/4 cup (20g) flaked pecorino

DILL LEMON DRESSING
1/4 cup (75g) mayonnaise
1 tablespoon lemon juice
1 tablespoon water
2 tablespoons finely chopped fresh dill

1 Combine ingredients for dill lemon dressing in screw-top jar; shake well.
2 Cook asparagus, in batches, on heated oiled grill plate (or grill or barbecue); chop coarsely.
3 Poach eggs; drain.
4 Divide spinach and asparagus among serving plates; top with an egg and a quarter of the cheese then drizzle spinach and asparagus with dressing.
per serving 12.9g total fat (3.1g saturated fat); 782kJ (187 cal); 5.4g carbohydrate; 11.6g protein; 2.7g fibre

thai herb and mango salad

PREPARATION TIME 25 MINUTES **SERVES** 4

2 medium mangoes (860g)
10cm stick (20g) fresh lemon grass,
  sliced thinly
2 fresh long red chillies, cut into thin strips
150g snow peas, trimmed, sliced thinly
6 green onions, sliced thinly
1 cup (80g) bean sprouts
$^1/_2$ cup loosely packed fresh coriander leaves
$^1/_4$ cup loosely packed fresh mint leaves
$^1/_4$ cup loosely packed
  vietnamese mint leaves
1 tablespoon coarsely shredded thai basil

PALM SUGAR AND LIME DRESSING
$^1/_4$ cup (60ml) lime juice
1 tablespoon fish sauce
2 tablespoons grated palm sugar
2 cloves garlic, crushed

1 Place ingredients for palm sugar and lime dressing in screw-top jar; shake well.
2 Slice cheeks from mangoes; cut each cheek into thin strips.
3 Combine mango in large bowl with remaining ingredients and dressing.
per serving 0.6g total fat (0g saturated fat); 631kJ (151 cal); 29.3g carbohydrate; 4.5g protein; 5g fibre

A MANGO'S BRILLIANT GOLDEN ORANGE, FRAGRANT FLESH TASTES OF THE TROPICS

Chorizo, a highly seasoned Spanish pork sausage, can be smoked or air-dried, and is as good grilled and eaten on its own as it is used as an ingredient, traditionally in an authentic paella.

chorizo, curly endive, orange and walnut salad

PREPARATION TIME 10 MINUTES
COOKING TIME 5 MINUTES **SERVES** 4

2 chorizo sausages (340g), sliced thinly
2 medium oranges (480g)
150g curly endive, trimmed
³/₄ cup (75g) roasted walnuts

WALNUT ORANGE DRESSING
¹/₄ cup (60ml) walnut oil
1 teaspoon finely grated orange rind
¹/₄ cup (60ml) orange juice
1 teaspoon dijon mustard

1 Combine ingredients for walnut orange dressing in screw-top jar; shake well.
2 Cook chorizo in large frying pan, stirring occasionally, until browned. Cool 10 minutes.
3 Segment oranges over large bowl. Add chorizo, endive, nuts and dressing to bowl; toss gently.

per serving 52.3g total fat (12.6g saturated fat); 2500kJ (598 cal); 10.9g carbohydrate; 20.7g protein; 4.2g fibre

roasted beetroot and potato with paprika mayonnaise

PREPARATION TIME 5 MINUTES
COOKING TIME 40 MINUTES **SERVES** 6

1 tablespoon olive oil
3 medium beetroots, peeled,
  cut into 3cm pieces
400g baby new potatoes
2 bacon rashers (140g), rind removed,
  chopped coarsely
100g baby rocket leaves, trimmed

PAPRIKA MAYONNAISE
¹/₂ cup (150g) mayonnaise
1 tablespoon lemon juice
4 sweet gherkins (35g), chopped coarsely
1 teaspoon sweet paprika
1 clove garlic, crushed

1 Preheat oven to moderately hot (200°C/180°C fan-forced).
2 Combine oil, beetroot and potatoes in large shallow baking dish. Roast, turning occasionally, about 30 minutes or until vegetables are almost tender.
3 Add bacon to dish; cook about 10 minutes or until bacon is crisp. Remove dish from oven; stand 10 minutes. Halve unpeeled potatoes; drain bacon.
4 Whisk ingredients for paprika mayonnaise in small bowl.
5 Toss rocket with vegetables and bacon; serve accompanied with mayonnaise.

per serving 13g total fat (2g saturated fat); 974kJ (233 cal); 21.2g carbohydrate; 6g protein; 3.9g fibre

French green lentils (sometimes known as Australian green lentils), grown in Victoria, are a local cousin to the expensive French import, lentils du puy. They have a sensational nutty, earthy flavour and hold up well when being boiled without disintegrating or becoming muddy.

warm lentil and chorizo salad

PREPARATION TIME 15 MINUTES
COOKING TIME 25 MINUTES **SERVES** 6

1¼ cups (250g) french green lentils
1 small brown onion (80g), quartered
1 bay leaf
2 chorizo sausages (340g), sliced thinly
3 shallots (75g), sliced thinly
2 trimmed celery stalks (200g),
  sliced diagonally
1 cup coarsely chopped fresh flat-leaf parsley

MACADAMIA DRESSING
½ cup (125ml) red wine vinegar
⅓ cup (80ml) macadamia oil

1 Cook lentils, onion and bay leaf in large saucepan of boiling water, uncovered, about 15 minutes or until lentils are tender; drain. Discard onion and bay leaf.
2 Cook chorizo in large frying pan, stirring occasionally, until browned. Drain; cool 10 minutes.
3 Combine ingredients for macadamia dressing in screw-top jar; shake well.
4 Combine lentils and chorizo in large bowl with shallot, celery, parsley and dressing.
per serving 30.2g total fat (8.1g saturated fat); 1860kJ (445 cal); 19.1g carbohydrate; 21.8g protein; 7.3g fibre

rösti stacks with prawns and mint aïoli

PREPARATION TIME 30 MINUTES
COOKING TIME 20 MINUTES **SERVES** 4

16 uncooked medium king prawns (720g)
800g russet burbank potatoes,
  grated coarsely
1 teaspoon finely chopped fresh rosemary
2 cloves garlic, crushed
2 tablespoons olive oil
30g baby rocket leaves

MINT AÏOLI
1/3 cup coarsely chopped fresh mint
1 clove garlic, quartered
1 egg
1 tablespoon dijon mustard
1/2 cup (125ml) olive oil

1 Make mint aïoli.
2 Shell and devein prawns, leaving tails intact.
3 To make rösti, squeeze excess moisture from potato; combine in medium bowl with rosemary and garlic. Divide into eight portions.
4 Heat half the oil in large frying pan; cook rösti, in batches, flattening slightly, until browned both sides. Drain.
5 Heat remaining oil in pan; cook prawns until just changed in colour.
6 Serve rösti stacked alternately with prawns, mint aïoli and rocket.
MINT AÏOLI Blend or process mint, garlic, egg and mustard until mixture is pureed. With motor operating, add oil in a thin, steady stream until aïoli thickens.
per serving 39.8g total fat (5.8g saturated fat); 2324kJ (556 cal); 23.6g carbohydrate; 24.9g protein; 3.7g fibre

RÖSTI, THE CLASSIC SWISS POTATO CAKE, IS BEST MADE FROM A STARCHY POTATO SUCH AS THE RUSSET BURBANK

We used a brie cheese here. It can be replaced with its blue-vein counterpart, if you prefer, but select one that's mild and very creamy.

shaved fennel and apple salad with brie and pecans

PREPARATION TIME 20 MINUTES **SERVES** 6

2 baby fennel (260g)
2 medium green apples (300g)
1 cup (120g) roasted pecans
150g brie, sliced thinly
1 red coral lettuce, trimmed,
  chopped coarsely

MUSTARD VINAIGRETTE
$^1/_3$ cup (80ml) olive oil
$^1/_4$ cup (60ml) lemon juice
1 tablespoon wholegrain mustard

1 Combine ingredients for mustard vinaigrette in screw-top jar; shake well.
2 Trim and halve fennel; reserve 2 tablespoons coarsely chopped frond-tips. Halve and core unpeeled apples. Using a very sharp knife, mandoline or V-slicer, slice fennel and apple thinly.
3 Combine fennel and apple in large bowl with frond tips, nuts, cheese and dressing; serve on top of lettuce.
per serving 33.3g total fat (6.8g saturated fat); 1496kJ (358 cal); 6.6g carbohydrate; 7.4g protein; 3.5g fibre

swiss brown mushroom and warm pancetta salad

PREPARATION TIME 10 MINUTES
COOKING TIME 10 MINUTES **SERVES** 6

200g swiss brown mushrooms, quartered
$^1/_4$ cup (60ml) balsamic vinegar
8 slices pancetta (120g)
100g baby spinach leaves, trimmed
2 tablespoons drained baby capers, rinsed
2 green onions, chopped finely
1 tablespoon olive oil
1 clove garlic, crushed

1 Combine mushrooms with 2 tablespoons of the vinegar in small bowl.
2 Cook pancetta in medium oiled frying pan until crisp; chop coarsely.
3 Drain mushrooms; discard vinegar. Cook mushrooms in same pan until tender.
4 Combine remaining ingredients in large bowl with pancetta, mushrooms and remaining vinegar.
per serving 6g total fat (1.5g saturated fat); 360kJ (86 cal); 1.3g carbohydrate; 5.6g protein; 1.6g fibre

Make sure you use prepared white horseradish in the dressing and not the blended condiment sold by the name of horseradish cream.

eggplant, fetta and semi-dried tomato salad

PREPARATION TIME 20 MINUTES
COOKING TIME 15 MINUTES **SERVES** 6

2 medium red capsicums (400g)
8 baby eggplants (480g), halved lengthways
1 medium red onion (170g), cut into wedges
250g fetta, crumbled
350g watercress, trimmed
100g drained semi-dried tomatoes,
   sliced thinly

CREAMY HORSERADISH DRESSING
1 egg
2 tablespoons prepared horseradish
2 teaspoons honey
2 cloves garlic, quartered
²/₃ cup (160ml) olive oil

1 Quarter capsicums; discard seeds and membranes. Cook capsicum, eggplant and onion, in batches, on heated oiled grill plate (or grill or barbecue) until browned. Cover capsicum pieces for 5 minutes; peel.
2 Make creamy horseradish dressing.
3 Combine cheese, watercress and tomato in medium bowl; divide among serving plates. Top with capsicum, eggplant and onion; drizzle with dressing.
CREAMY HORSERADISH DRESSING Blend or process egg, horseradish, honey and garlic until smooth. With motor operating, add oil in thin, steady stream until dressing thickens slightly.
per serving 36.3g total fat (10.2g saturated fat); 1910kJ (457 cal); 14.6g carbohydrate; 15.1g protein; 8.2g fibre

Fried "crisp" noodles, commonly used in chow mein and sang choy bow, are deep-fried wheat noodles found on supermarket shelves packaged in 50g or 100g lots.

smoked chicken chow-mein salad with raspberry macadamia dressing

PREPARATION TIME 20 MINUTES **SERVES** 6

100g packet fried noodles
$^1/_2$ cup (70g) roasted macadamias, chopped coarsely
100g baby rocket leaves
100g mizuna
1 small red onion (100g), sliced thinly
$^1/_2$ cup firmly packed fresh flat-leaf parsley leaves
$^1/_2$ cup firmly packed fresh mint leaves
800g smoked chicken breast fillets, sliced thinly

RASPBERRY MACADAMIA DRESSING
2 cloves garlic, crushed
$^1/_4$ cup (60ml) raspberry vinegar
1 tablespoon wholegrain mustard
$^1/_3$ cup (80ml) macadamia oil

1 Combine ingredients for raspberry macadamia dressing in screw-top jar; shake well.
2 Combine salad ingredients in large bowl with dressing.
per serving 32.3g total fat (6.3g saturated fat); 1923kJ (460 cal); 5.8g carbohydrate; 35.5g protein; 2.8g fibre

Carpaccio, usually served in Italy as a "primi piatti" (literally, the first plate), a first-course salad, can be made with finely sliced fish as well as the traditional beef fillet. Be certain that the meat you buy is as fresh as possible and from a reliable source.

carpaccio with shaved parmesan and basil salsa verde

PREPARATION TIME 30 MINUTES (PLUS FREEZING TIME) **SERVES** 6

400g piece beef fillet, trimmed
1 baby cos lettuce, trimmed, shredded finely
40g parmesan, shaved finely

BASIL SALSA VERDE
$^1/_2$ cup finely chopped fresh flat-leaf parsley
$^1/_4$ cup finely chopped fresh basil
2 tablespoons finely chopped fresh mint
4 anchovy fillets, drained, chopped finely
1 tablespoon drained capers, rinsed,
   chopped finely
1 clove garlic, crushed
2 teaspoons dijon mustard
2 tablespoons red wine vinegar
$^1/_3$ cup (80ml) olive oil

1 Enclose beef tightly in plastic wrap; freeze about 1 hour or until partially frozen. Slice beef as thinly as possible.
2 Combine ingredients for basil salsa verde in small bowl.
3 Arrange beef on serving plates in a single layer; top with lettuce and cheese. Spoon salsa verde over beef.
per serving 18.7g total fat (4.8g saturated fat); 1028kJ (246 cal); 1g carbohydrate; 18g protein; 1.3g fibre

Hot-smoked ocean trout can be found, cryovac-packed, in the refrigerated section of supermarkets and at fish shops. If unavailable, use cold-smoked trout.

smoked trout, peach and watercress salad with lemon buttermilk dressing

PREPARATION TIME 10 MINUTES **SERVES** 4

600g piece hot-smoked ocean trout
200g watercress, trimmed
2 medium peaches (460g),
   cut into thin wedges

LEMON BUTTERMILK DRESSING
$^1/_4$ cup (60ml) buttermilk
1 tablespoon lemon juice
1 teaspoon finely grated lemon rind
1 teaspoon white sugar

1 Combine ingredients for lemon buttermilk dressing in screw-top jar; shake well.
2 Discard skin and bones from fish; break fish into large pieces in medium bowl. Add watercress and peach; toss gently. Serve salad drizzled with dressing.
per serving 8.1g total fat (2g saturated fat); 1170kJ (280 cal); 8.7g carbohydrate; 40.7g protein; 3.3g fibre

barbecued pork and crunchy noodle salad

PREPARATION TIME 20 MINUTES **SERVES** 6

10 trimmed red radishes (150g),
  sliced thinly, cut into matchsticks
1 large red capsicum (350g) sliced thinly
2 baby buk choy (300g), sliced thinly
6 green onions, sliced thinly
1 cup (80g) bean sprouts
$^1/_2$ cup (70g) roasted slivered almonds
2 x 100g packets fried noodles
400g chinese barbecued pork, sliced thinly

SWEET-SOUR DRESSING
$^1/_4$ cup (60ml) peanut oil
2 tablespoons white vinegar
2 tablespoons brown sugar
2 tablespoons light soy sauce
1 teaspoon sesame oil
1 clove garlic, crushed

1 Combine ingredients for sweet-sour dressing in screw-top jar; shake well.
2 Combine salad ingredients in large bowl with dressing.
per serving 29.7g total fat (7.6g saturated fat); 1789kJ (428 cal); 17.6g carbohydrate; 20.4g protein; 6.1g fibre

Tuna sold as sashimi has to meet stringent guidelines regarding its handling and treatment after leaving the water, but it is still probably a good idea to buy it only from a fishmonger you trust or to seek advice from local authorities before eating any raw seafood.

tuna tartare on baby cos

PREPARATION TIME 25 MINUTES (PLUS REFRIGERATION TIME)
SERVES 6

200g piece sashimi tuna, trimmed
1 tablespoon drained capers, rinsed,
   chopped finely
2 teaspoons prepared horseradish
$^1/_3$ cup (80ml) lime juice
2 small tomatoes (180g), seeded,
   chopped finely
1 small avocado (200g), chopped finely
1 small red onion (100g), chopped finely
1 baby cos lettuce, trimmed, leaves separated
1 tablespoon extra virgin olive oil

1   Cut tuna into 5mm pieces; combine in medium bowl with capers, horseradish and 1 tablespoon of the juice. Cover; refrigerate 30 minutes.
2   Combine tomato, avocado, onion and remaining juice in medium bowl.
3   Serve lettuce leaves topped with tomato mixture and tuna tartare, drizzled with oil.
per serving 10.4g total fat (2.3g saturated fat); 610kJ (146cal); 2.4g carbohydrate; 9.8g protein; 1.6g fibre

goat cheese, fig and prosciutto salad

PREPARATION TIME 10 MINUTES
COOKING TIME 5 MINUTES **SERVES** 4

6 slices prosciutto (90g)
120g baby rocket leaves, trimmed
4 large fresh figs (320g), quartered
150g soft goat cheese, crumbled

HONEY CIDER DRESSING
$^1/_4$ cup (60ml) cider vinegar
2 tablespoons olive oil
1 tablespoon wholegrain mustard
1 tablespoon honey

1 Preheat grill.
2 Combine ingredients for honey cider dressing in screw-top jar; shake well.
3 Crisp prosciutto under grill; drain, chop coarsely.
4 Serve rocket topped with fig, cheese and prosciutto; drizzle with dressing.
TIP Freeze cheese for 10 minutes to make crumbling easier.
per serving 16.9g total fat (5.7g saturated fat); 1062kJ (254 cal); 13.7g carbohydrate; 11.1g protein; 2.6g fibre

turkish haloumi and pomegranate salad

PREPARATION TIME 15 MINUTES
COOKING TIME 5 MINUTES **SERVES** 4

1 tablespoon lemon juice
2 tablespoons light olive oil
$^1/_3$ cup (80ml) pomegranate pulp
$^1/_4$ cup firmly packed fresh mint leaves
2 green onions, sliced thinly
125g mizuna
1 medium fennel (300g), trimmed,
  sliced thinly
360g haloumi cheese, sliced thickly

1 Combine juice, oil, pulp, mint, onion, mizuna and fennel in large bowl.
2 Brown cheese, both sides, in large oiled frying pan. Serve salad topped with cheese.
per serving 24.7g total fat (11.2g saturated fat); 1400kJ (335 cal); 6.5g carbohydrate; 20.6g protein; 3.5g fibre

ONE LARGE POMEGRANATE WILL HOLD ENOUGH SWEET-SOUR PULP FOR THIS RECIPE

chilli, salt and pepper squid salad

PREPARATION TIME 35 MINUTES
COOKING TIME 10 MINUTES **SERVES** 4

600g cleaned squid hoods
$^1/_4$ cup (35g) plain flour
1 fresh long red chilli, chopped finely
1 teaspoon sea salt flakes
$^1/_2$ teaspoon cracked black pepper
vegetable oil, for deep-frying
50g mesclun
1 small red capsicum (150g), sliced thinly
1 lebanese cucumber (130g), sliced thinly
$^1/_3$ cup loosely packed fresh coriander leaves
2 teaspoons olive oil
1 medium lemon (140g), cut into wedges

1 Cut squid down centre to open out; score the inside in a diagonal pattern. Halve squid lengthways; cut each piece in half crossways.
2 Combine flour, chilli, salt and pepper in medium bowl; add squid, toss to coat in flour mixture. Shake away excess.
3 Heat vegetable oil in wok; deep-fry squid, in batches, until tender. Drain.
4 Combine mesclun, capsicum, cucumber, coriander and olive oil in large bowl with warm squid. Serve with lemon.
per serving 12.6g total fat (2g saturated fat); 1112kJ (266 cal); 9g carbohydrate; 27g protein; 2.3g fibre

LONG RED CHILLIES ARE GENERALLY MILDER THAN THE SMALLER INCENDIARY BIRD'S-EYE VARIETY

An Italian gremolata is traditionally a blend of finely chopped lemon rind, parsley and garlic, usually sprinkled over osso buco just before serving to enliven the tastebuds. This tempting twist on the classic calls for orange rather than lemon.

char-grilled scallop and witlof salad with orange gremolata

PREPARATION TIME 10 MINUTES
COOKING TIME 10 MINUTES **SERVES** 4

2 red witlof (250g), quartered
16 scallops (400g) roe removed

ORANGE DRESSING
2 tablespoons olive oil
1 tablespoon orange juice

ORANGE GREMOLATA
1/4 cup finely chopped fresh flat-leaf parsley
1 tablespoon finely grated orange rind
1 clove garlic, crushed

1 Combine ingredients for orange dressing in small jug.
2 Combine ingredients for orange gremolata in small bowl.
3 Cook witlof on heated oiled grill plate (or grill or barbecue) until browned lightly.
4 Cook scallops on grill plate until cooked.
5 Drizzle witlof and scallops with dressing and serve accompanied with gremolata.
per serving 9.9g total fat (1.5g saturated fat); 615kJ (147 cal); 1.7g carbohydrate; 12.3g protein; 1.4g fibre

CLASSIC SALADS HAVE STOOD THE TEST OF TIME. YET, AS EVERY NEW GENERATION DISCOVERS THEM, SUBTLE CHANGES ARE MADE

The original French salade niçoise was created with the finest local produce from Provence — vine-ripened tomatoes, piquant caperberries, tiny, firm black olives, hand-picked baby beans and fresh tuna caught just off the coast. Our version has adapted a modern approach more suitable to our hectic lifestyle; if you wish, however, instead of using canned tuna, char-grill four 200g tuna steaks briefly and centre one of them on each beautiful salad arrangement.

salade niçoise

PREPARATION TIME 15 MINUTES
COOKING TIME 5 MINUTES **SERVES** 4

200g baby green beans, trimmed
2 tablespoons olive oil
1 tablespoon lemon juice
2 tablespoons white wine vinegar
4 medium tomatoes (600g), cut into wedges
4 hard-boiled eggs, quartered
425g can tuna in springwater, drained, flaked
½ cup (80g) drained caperberries, rinsed
½ cup (60g) seeded small black olives
¼ cup firmly packed fresh flat-leaf parsley leaves
440g can drained whole baby new potatoes,
  rinsed, halved

1 Boil, steam or microwave beans until tender; drain. Rinse under cold water; drain.
2 Whisk oil, juice and vinegar in large bowl; add beans and remaining ingredients, mix gently.
per serving 16.9g total fat (3.7g saturated fat); 1522kJ (364 cal); 19.5g carbohydrate; 30.9g protein; 5.2g fibre

Everyone has a different opinion as to what a potato salad should be – served hot or cold, creamy or dressed with a vinaigrette, with bacon bits or simply sprinkled with fresh herbs – but you'd be hard-pressed to find one you didn't like. Cover the saucepan while potatoes are cooking, but lift the lid and give them an occasional gentle stir to move them around. Don't overcook them or they will break apart or crumble.

potato

PREPARATION TIME 30 MINUTES (PLUS REFRIGERATION TIME)
COOKING TIME 15 MINUTES **SERVES** 8

2kg potatoes, peeled
2 tablespoons cider vinegar
4 green onions, sliced thinly
$^1/_4$ cup finely chopped fresh flat-leaf parsley

MAYONNAISE
2 egg yolks
2 teaspoons lemon juice
1 teaspoon dijon mustard
1 cup (250ml) vegetable oil
2 tablespoons warm water, approximately

1 Cover potatoes with cold water in large saucepan; bring to a boil. Reduce heat; simmer, covered, until tender. Drain; cut into 3cm pieces. Spread potato on a tray, sprinkle with vinegar; refrigerate until cold.
2 Make mayonnaise.
3 Combine potato in large bowl with mayonnaise, onion and parsley.
MAYONNAISE Blend or process egg yolks, juice and mustard until smooth. With motor operating, gradually add oil in a thin, steady stream; process until mixture thickens. Add as much of the warm water as required to thin mayonnaise.
per serving 30.4g total fat (4.1g saturated fat); 1764kJ (422 cal); 29g carbohydrate; 6.2g protein; 3.7g fibre

PROPERLY COOKED, ANY WAXY, WHITE-FLESHED POTATO WILL HOLD ITS SHAPE WHEN TOSSED IN A SALAD

Tabbouleh is traditionally made with a great deal of chopped flat-leaf parsley and varying smaller amounts of burghul, green onion and mint. Go easy on the burghul: too much and the completed tabbouleh will be overly heavy instead of fluffy and light as it is meant to be.

tabbouleh

PREPARATION TIME 30 MINUTES (PLUS REFRIGERATION TIME)
SERVES 4

$^1/_4$ cup (40g) burghul
3 medium tomatoes (450g)
3 cups coarsely chopped
  fresh flat-leaf parsley
3 green onions, chopped finely
$^1/_4$ cup coarsely chopped fresh mint
$^1/_4$ cup (60ml) lemon juice
$^1/_4$ cup (60ml) olive oil

1 Place burghul in medium shallow bowl. Halve tomatoes, scoop pulp from tomato over burghul. Chop tomato flesh finely; spread over burghul. Cover; refrigerate 1 hour.
2 Combine burghul mixture in large bowl with remaining ingredients.
per serving 14.1g total fat (2g saturated fat); 790kJ (189 cal); 9.2g carbohydrate; 3.4g protein; 5.6g fibre

This crunchy salad is found on tables all over the world, not just in Greece. The only obligatory ingredients are fetta, tomato and onion; use your imagination and add capers, hard-boiled eggs, and red or green capsicum — as long as it offers "bite", the sky's the limit.

greek

PREPARATION TIME 15 MINUTES **SERVES** 4

4 medium egg tomatoes (300g),
  sliced thinly
2 lebanese cucumbers (260g),
  chopped coarsely
1 small red onion (100g), sliced thinly
$^1/_2$ cup (75g) seeded kalamata olives
150g fetta, chopped coarsely
2 tablespoons olive oil
2 tablespoons lemon juice
2 teaspoons fresh oregano leaves

1 Combine tomato, cucumber, onion, olives and cheese in large bowl.
2 Combine remaining ingredients in screw-top jar; shake well. Drizzle dressing over salad.
per serving 18.2g total fat (7.1g saturated fat); 991kJ (237 cal); 9g carbohydrate; 8.3g protein; 2.4g fibre

Named after Caesar Cardini, the Italian-American who tossed the first caesar in Mexico during the 1920s, this salad always contains fresh croutons, crisp cos lettuce leaves, lightly boiled eggs, lemon juice, olive oil, worcestershire and parmesan but no one ingredient should dominate.

caesar

PREPARATION TIME 30 MINUTES
COOKING TIME 15 MINUTES **SERVES** 4

¹/₂ loaf ciabatta (220g)
1 clove garlic, crushed
¹/₃ cup (80ml) olive oil
2 eggs
3 baby cos lettuces, trimmed,
  leaves separated
1 cup (80g) flaked parmesan

CAESAR DRESSING
1 clove garlic, crushed
1 tablespoon dijon mustard
2 tablespoons lemon juice
2 teaspoons worcestershire sauce
2 tablespoons olive oil

1 Preheat oven to moderate (180°C/160°C fan-forced).
2 Cut bread into 2cm cubes; combine garlic and oil in large bowl with bread. Toast bread on oven tray until croutons are browned.
3 Combine ingredients for caesar dressing in screw-top jar; shake well.
4 Bring water to a boil in small saucepan, add eggs; cover pan tightly, remove from heat. Remove eggs from water after 2 minutes. When cool enough to handle, break eggs into large bowl; add lettuce, mixing gently so egg coats leaves.
5 Add cheese, croutons and dressing to bowl; toss gently.
per serving 39.1g total fat (9.1g saturated fat); 2366kJ (566 cal); 33.1g carbohydrate; 18.4g protein; 5.6g fibre

You can use any cabbage variety for coleslaw – red, savoy, even wombok – but we chose to shred a traditional firm, white drumhead in our recipe. After trimming a cabbage, cut it into manageable-size wedges to make shredding it finely a lot easier.

coleslaw

PREPARATION TIME 10 MINUTES **SERVES** 6

$^1/_2$ small cabbage (600g), shredded finely
1 medium carrot (120g), grated coarsely
4 green onions, sliced thinly
$^1/_2$ cup (150g) mayonnaise
1 tablespoon lemon juice

1 Combine ingredients in large bowl.
per serving 8.1g total fat (1g saturated fat); 523kJ (125 cal); 8.8g carbohydrate; 2g protein; 4.5g fibre

In recent years, the Western world has embraced Thai cuisine with great enthusiasm and this char-grilled salad, found on Thai menus under the name of yum nuah, deliciously explains why.

thai beef

PREPARATION TIME 15 MINUTES (PLUS REFRIGERATION TIME)
COOKING TIME 10 MINUTES **SERVES** 4

500g beef rump steak
$^1/_4$ cup (60ml) fish sauce
$^1/_4$ cup (60ml) lime juice
1 tablespoon grated palm sugar
2 teaspoons light soy sauce
1 clove garlic, crushed
3 lebanese cucumbers (390g),
   seeded, sliced thinly
4 fresh small red thai chillies, sliced thinly
8 green onions, sliced thinly
250g cherry tomatoes, quartered
1 cup loosely packed vietnamese mint leaves
1 cup loosely packed fresh coriander leaves

1 Combine beef, 2 tablespoons of the fish sauce and 1 tablespoon of the juice in large bowl; refrigerate 3 hours or overnight.
2 Drain beef; discard marinade. Cook beef on heated oiled grill plate (or grill or barbecue). Cover; stand 5 minutes then slice thinly.
3 Whisk remaining fish sauce and juice with sugar, soy sauce and garlic in large bowl. Add beef, cucumber, chilli, onion, tomato and herbs; mix gently.
per serving 8.8g total fat (3.8g saturated fat); 1062kJ (254 cal); 9.6g carbohydrate; 31.4g protein; 4.2g fibre

Pasta salad is another one of those favourites that has as many versions as there are cooks who make it. Because it's eaten cold, it's ideal for picnics or lunchboxes, and as a side salad with a simple midweek meal of grilled chops.

pasta

PREPARATION TIME 15 MINUTES
COOKING TIME 10 MINUTES SERVES 4

250g orecchiette
2 tablespoons drained sun-dried
   tomatoes, chopped coarsely
1 small red onion (100g), sliced thinly
1 small green capsicum (150g), sliced thinly
1/2 cup coarsely chopped fresh
   flat-leaf parsley

SUN-DRIED TOMATO DRESSING
1 tablespoon sun-dried tomato pesto
1 tablespoon white wine vinegar
2 tablespoons olive oil

1   Cook pasta in large saucepan of boiling water, uncovered, until just tender; drain. Rinse under cold water; drain.
2   Combine ingredients for sun-dried tomato dressing in screw-top jar; shake well.
3   Combine pasta in large bowl with remaining ingredients and dressing; toss gently.

per serving 12g total fat (1.9g saturated fat); 1405kJ (336 cal); 46g carbohydrate; 8.8g protein; 3.6g fibre

IF YOU CAN'T FIND ORECCHIETTE, REPLACE IT WITH PENNE, THE QUILL-SHAPED PASTA

This simple salad is native to Campania, the largely agricultural region of Italy that's also the home of "mozzarella di bufala", the fresh stretched buffalo milk cheese that's an important component of a classic caprese. It's said that the ingredients of a caprese are meant to represent the colours of the Italian flag: bright red tomato, milky white mozzarella and the sharp green of basil. Buffalo mozzarella is available locally, but it can be hard to find and expensive, so we used fresh, good-quality bocconcini here with great results.

caprese

PREPARATION TIME 15 MINUTES **SERVES** 4

3 large egg tomatoes (270g), sliced thinly
300g bocconcini, drained, sliced thinly
2 tablespoons olive oil
1/4 cup firmly packed fresh basil leaves, torn

1   Overlap slices of tomato and cheese on serving platter.
2   Drizzle with oil; sprinkle with basil.
per serving 20.6g total fat (8.8g saturated fat); 1028kJ (246 cal); 1.6g carbohydrate; 13.6g protein; 1.1g fibre

A signature dish from the kitchen of New York's world-famous Waldorf-Astoria hotel, the Waldorf salad was created at the beginning of the 20th century, and proved so popular that it rapidly became a staple in kitchens throughout America.

waldorf

PREPARATION TIME 15 MINUTES **SERVES** 4

4 medium red apples (600g)
1/4 cup (60ml) lemon juice
5 trimmed celery stalks (500g), chopped coarsely
1 cup (110g) coarsely chopped roasted walnuts

MAYONNAISE
2 egg yolks
2 teaspoons lemon juice
1 teaspoon dijon mustard
3/4 cup (180ml) olive oil
1 tablespoon warm water

1   Make mayonnaise.
2   Core unpeeled apples; cut into thin wedges. Combine in large serving bowl with juice, celery, nuts and mayonnaise.
MAYONNAISE Blend or process egg yolks, juice and mustard until smooth. With motor operating, gradually add oil in a thin, steady stream; process until mixture thickens. Add as much of the warm water as required to thin mayonnaise.
per serving 63.1g total fat (7.8g saturated fat); 2800kJ (670 cal); 17.8g carbohydrate; 6.8g protein; 6.5g fibre

MAIN-COURSE SALADS CAN BE ELEGANT ENOUGH FOR A DINNER PARTY OR SERVED AS A SIMPLE MEAL EATEN FROM A BOWL

Preserved lemon (pictured above) is a North African speciality, where lemons, whole or sliced, are placed in a mixture of salt and oil or lemon juice. Rinsed well, the peel can be chopped and stirred into a salad dressing, or added to a simmering casserole or tagine for extra piquancy.

moroccan couscous salad with preserved lemon dressing

PREPARATION TIME 20 MINUTES **SERVES** 4

1¹/₂ cups (300g) couscous
1¹/₂ cups (375ml) boiling water
20g butter
420g can chickpeas, rinsed, drained
¹/₃ cup (55g) sultanas
¹/₃ cup (50g) roasted pine nuts
100g baby rocket leaves, chopped coarsely
³/₄ cup finely chopped fresh flat-leaf parsley
1 cup (120g) seeded green olives

PRESERVED LEMON DRESSING
1 tablespoon finely grated lemon rind
¹/₄ cup (60ml) lemon juice
¹/₄ cup (60ml) olive oil
2 tablespoons rinsed and drained
   finely chopped preserved lemon

1 Combine couscous with the water in large heatproof bowl, cover; stand about 5 minutes or until water is absorbed, fluffing with fork occasionally. Stir in butter. Stand 10 minutes.
2 Combine ingredients for preserved lemon dressing in screw-top jar; shake well.
3 Combine couscous in large bowl with remaining ingredients and dressing.
per serving 29g total fat (5.5g saturated fat); 268kJ (686 cal); 85.6g carbohydrate; 17.2g protein; 6.5g fibre

Farfalle is a short, rather sturdy butterfly-shaped pasta that is also known as "bow-ties". It is good for a dish such as this because the folds and crinkles of each piece help capture the pesto and hold the other ingredients. Replace the farfalle with penne or small shells if you wish.

poached salmon and pasta salad with rocket pesto

PREPARATION TIME 25 MINUTES
COOKING TIME 25 MINUTES **SERVES** 6

500g farfalle
800g salmon fillets
1.25 litres (5 cups) water
$^1/_2$ medium lemon (70g), cut into wedges
1 small red onion (100g), sliced thinly
2 tablespoons drained capers, rinsed
2 medium tomatoes (300g), seeded, chopped finely
1 lebanese cucumber (130g), seeded, chopped finely
1 tablespoon finely grated lemon rind
$^1/_3$ cup (80ml) lemon juice

ROCKET PESTO
250g rocket, trimmed
$^1/_4$ cup (20g) coarsely grated parmesan
$^1/_4$ cup (40g) roasted pine nuts
2 cloves garlic, quartered
$^1/_2$ cup (125ml) olive oil

1 Make rocket pesto.
2 Cook pasta in large saucepan of boiling water, uncovered, until just tender; drain.
3 Halve fish fillets. Combine the water and lemon in large frying pan; bring to a boil. Add fish; simmer, uncovered, until fish is cooked, drain. Cut fish into chunks.
4 Combine pasta in large bowl with onion, capers, tomato, cucumber, rind and juice. Add fish and pesto; toss gently.
ROCKET PESTO Blend or process rocket, cheese, nuts and garlic until smooth. With motor operating, add oil in a thin, steady stream until pesto thickens.
per serving 35.6g total fat (6g saturated fat); 3089kJ (739 cal); 61.5g carbohydrate; 39.7g protein; 5.4g fibre

THE LEBANESE CUCUMBER IS A VERY POPULAR VARIETY BECAUSE OF ITS TINY SEEDS AND SWEET, FRESH TASTE

thai-style green mango salad with seared tuna

PREPARATION TIME 20 MINUTES
COOKING TIME 10 MINUTES **SERVES** 4

1 green mango (350g)
2 teaspoons sesame oil
800g tuna steaks, cut into 3cm pieces
$^1/_2$ teaspoon dried chilli flakes
2 tablespoons roasted sesame seeds
2 cups (100g) snow pea sprouts
$^1/_2$ cup firmly packed fresh coriander leaves
$^1/_2$ cup firmly packed fresh mint leaves
$^1/_2$ small red onion (50g), sliced thinly

LIME AND GINGER DRESSING
$^1/_4$ cup (60ml) lime juice
3cm piece fresh ginger (15g), grated
1 tablespoon fish sauce

1 Combine ingredients for lime and ginger dressing in screw-top jar; shake well.
2 Using vegetable peeler, slice mango into thin ribbons.
3 Combine oil and fish in medium bowl. Cook fish on heated oiled grill plate (or grill or barbecue).
4 Return fish to same cleaned bowl with chilli and seeds; mix gently.
5 Combine remaining ingredients and dressing in medium bowl. Serve salad topped with fish.

per serving 17.8g total fat (5.4g saturated fat); 1894kJ (453 cal); 15.5g carbohydrate; 55.5g protein; 3.7g fibre

Craisins are dried sweetened cranberries. They can be used in cooking sweet or savoury dishes or, as here, raw in a salad.

turkey, craisins and peanut salad in butter lettuce leaves

PREPARATION TIME 30 MINUTES (PLUS COOLING TIME)
COOKING TIME 40 MINUTES **SERVES** 6

1.5kg boneless turkey breast
1.5 litres (6 cups) water
$^1/_2$ cup (125ml) red wine vinegar
1 teaspoon dijon mustard
$^1/_4$ cup (60ml) light olive oil
$^2/_3$ cup (90g) craisins
3 trimmed celery stalks (300g), sliced thinly
$1^1/_4$ cups (100g) bean sprouts
1 cup (50g) snow pea sprouts
$^1/_2$ cup (70g) roasted unsalted peanuts
$^1/_2$ cup firmly packed fresh mint leaves, torn
1 butter lettuce, leaves separated

1 Cut turkey into three equal-sized pieces. Bring the water to a boil in large saucepan; add turkey. Simmer, covered, about 35 minutes or until turkey is cooked. Cool turkey in poaching liquid 15 minutes. Drain turkey; shred coarsely.
2 Combine vinegar, mustard and oil in large bowl. Add turkey, craisins, celery, sprouts, nuts and mint; toss gently. Serve salad with lettuce leaves.

per serving 23.1g total fat (4.1g saturated fat); 2019kJ (483 cal); 6.7g carbohydrate; 59.7g protein; 4.2g fibre

Elongated, with pale green, crinkly leaves, wombok (also known as chinese cabbage) is the most common cabbage used throughout South-East Asia. It can be shredded or chopped and eaten raw, braised, steamed or stir-fried. You need about half a small wombok for this recipe, a quarter of a savoy cabbage and a quarter of a red cabbage.

three-cabbage coleslaw with shredded chicken

PREPARATION TIME 20 MINUTES (PLUS REFRIGERATION TIME)
SERVES 6

3 cups (480g) shredded barbecued chicken
3 cups (240g) finely shredded wombok
3 cups (240g) finely shredded savoy cabbage
3 cups (240g) finely shredded red cabbage
2 medium carrots (240g), grated coarsely
1 medium green capsicum (200g),
 sliced thinly
¼ cup finely chopped fresh dill

FENNEL SLAW DRESSING
½ cup (140g) yogurt
⅓ cup (100g) mayonnaise
⅓ cup (80ml) cider vinegar
1 small brown onion (80g), grated coarsely
2 teaspoons white sugar
2 teaspoons fennel seeds

1   Combine ingredients for fennel slaw dressing in small bowl.
2   Combine salad ingredients in large bowl with dressing; mix gently. Refrigerate, covered, at least 1 hour.
per serving 12.4g total fat (2.9g saturated fat); 1095kJ (262 cal); 11.3g carbohydrate; 23.7g protein; 5g fibre

A LARGE BARBECUED CHICKEN WILL SUPPLY THE RIGHT AMOUNT OF SHREDDED MEAT FOR THIS RECIPE

black grape, chicken and wild rice salad with tarragon dressing

PREPARATION TIME 20 MINUTES
COOKING TIME 25 MINUTES **SERVES** 4

1 litre (4 cups) water
800g chicken breast fillets
1¹/₂ cups (300g) wild rice blend
²/₃ cup (110g) roasted blanched almonds
1 cup (190g) black grapes
¹/₄ cup loosely packed fresh tarragon leaves
2 green onions, sliced finely
2 teaspoons finely grated lemon rind
1 tablespoon lemon juice

TARRAGON DRESSING
¹/₂ cup (120g) sour cream
1 tablespoon dijon mustard
1 tablespoon finely chopped fresh tarragon
1 tablespoon water
2 teaspoons lemon juice

1 Bring the water to a boil in large frying pan; add chicken. Simmer, covered, about 10 minutes or until chicken is cooked. Cool chicken in poaching liquid 10 minutes; drain, slice thickly.
2 Cook rice in large saucepan of boiling water, uncovered, until tender; drain. Cool 10 minutes.
3 Combine ingredients for tarragon dressing in small bowl.
4 Combine rice in large bowl with nuts, grapes, tarragon, onion, rind and juice. Serve rice salad topped with chicken, accompanied with dressing.
per serving 32.1g total fat (10g saturated fat); 2575kJ (616 cal); 24.4g carbohydrate; 55.3g protein; 4.5g fibre

You need to buy a large chinese barbecued duck from your local Asian barbecued meat shop and a small bunch of silver beet for this recipe. Some greengrocers sell silver beet as spinach, but it is easily distinguished by its really thick white stems and large, stiff, crinkly leaves.

crisp-fried duck with mango and chilli-lime green salad

PREPARATION TIME 20 MINUTES
COOKING TIME 10 MINUTES **SERVES** 4

¹/₄ cup (60ml) lime juice
1 tablespoon sweet chilli sauce
1kg chinese barbecued duck
2 teaspoons peanut oil
500g silver beet, trimmed, chopped coarsely
1 cup loosely packed fresh coriander leaves
3 cups (240g) bean sprouts
1 medium mango (430g), sliced thinly
2 limes, cut into wedges

1 Combine juice and sauce in small jug.
2 Remove skin then meat from duck; discard bones, slice skin thinly.
3 Heat oil in wok; stir-fry skin until crisp. Drain. Slice duck meat thinly; stir-fry until hot.
4 Combine silver beet, coriander, sprouts, mango, duck and juice mixture in large bowl; toss gently. Sprinkle salad with slivered duck skin, serve with lime wedges.

per serving 39.8g total fat (11.6g saturated fat); 2261kJ (541 cal); 12.5g carbohydrate; 31.8g protein; 4.7g fibre

crunchy snow pea, prawn and avocado salad with chive vinaigrette

PREPARATION TIME 20 MINUTES
COOKING TIME 5 MINUTES **SERVES** 4

750g cooked medium king prawns
150g sugar snap peas, trimmed
3 small avocados (600g), sliced thickly
2 cups (100g) snow pea sprouts

CHIVE VINAIGRETTE
¹/₄ cup (60ml) white wine vinegar
¹/₄ cup (60ml) olive oil
¹/₄ cup finely chopped fresh chives

1 Combine ingredients for chive vinaigrette in small bowl.
2 Shell and devein prawns, leaving tails intact.
3 Boil, steam or microwave peas until just tender; rinse under cold water, drain.
4 Combine peas in large bowl with prawns, avocado, sprouts and vinaigrette; toss gently.

per serving 38.2g total fat (7.2g saturated fat); 1998kJ (478 cal); 8.2g carbohydrate; 24.6g protein; 3.7g fibre

Pappadums, dried cracker-like wafers made from lentil and rice flours, must be reconstituted before they are eaten. We do this the low-fat way, giving them a burst in a microwave oven, but they are usually deep-fried to make them puff up and double in size. We used large plain pappadums here, but there are many sizes and flavour combinations to choose from.

tandoori chicken, spinach and mint salad with spiced yogurt

PREPARATION TIME 20 MINUTES (PLUS REFRIGERATION TIME)
COOKING TIME 15 MINUTES **SERVES** 4

1/3 cup (100g) tandoori paste
1/4 cup (70g) yogurt
800g chicken tenderloins
1 tablespoon vegetable oil
8 large uncooked pappadums
150g baby spinach leaves, trimmed
2 lebanese cucumbers (260g),
  sliced thickly
250g cherry tomatoes, halved
1 cup firmly packed fresh mint leaves

SPICED YOGURT
1 clove garlic, crushed
3/4 cup (210g) yogurt
1 tablespoon lemon juice
1 teaspoon ground cumin
1 teaspoon ground coriander

1 Combine paste and yogurt in medium bowl with chicken. Cover; refrigerate 3 hours or overnight.
2 Combine ingredients for spiced yogurt in small jug.
3 Heat oil in large frying pan; cook chicken, in batches, until cooked through.
4 Microwave 2 pappadums at a time on HIGH (100%) about 30 seconds.
5 Combine chicken in large bowl with spinach, cucumber, tomato and mint. Drizzle with yogurt; serve with pappadums.
per serving 12.5g total fat (3.4g saturated fat); 1731kJ (414 cal); 16.4g carbohydrate; 55.1g protein; 6.7g fibre

Larb is a classic Thai salad usually made with spiced minced beef, chicken or pork served with raw herbs and vegetables. This version is made with the vegetarian's "meat", tofu, with no lessening of fabulous flavour. Be careful when deep-frying the tofu because it can splatter.

larb tofu

PREPARATION TIME 20 MINUTES (PLUS STANDING TIME)
COOKING TIME 30 MINUTES **SERVES** 4

900g fresh firm silken tofu
1 cup (200g) rice flour
peanut oil, for deep-frying
1 medium red onion (170g), chopped finely
1/2 cup coarsely chopped fresh coriander
10cm stick (20g) fresh lemon grass,
  chopped finely
1 fresh long red chilli, chopped finely
1 teaspoon grated palm sugar
2 tablespoons lemon juice
1 tablespoon light soy sauce
1/2 teaspoon sambal oelek
8 wombok leaves

1 Dry tofu with absorbent paper then chop coarsely. Stand tofu on several layers of absorbent paper, cover with more paper; stand 20 minutes.
2 Toss tofu in rice flour; shake off excess.
3 Heat oil in wok; deep-fry tofu, in batches, until browned lightly. Drain on absorbent paper.
4 Combine tofu in large bowl with onion, coriander, lemon grass and chilli.
5 Dissolve sugar in juice in small jug; stir in sauce and sambal. Pour enough dressing over larb to just moisten; toss gently to combine.
6 Serve larb in individual leaves accompanied with any remaining dressing.
per serving 27.8g total fat (4.5g saturated fat); 1714kJ (410 cal); 8.4g carbohydrate; 29.2g protein; 6.5g fibre

YOU NEED HALF A SMALL WOMBOK (ALSO KNOWN AS CHINESE CABBAGE) FOR THIS RECIPE

ruby red grapefruit, smoked salmon and mizuna

PREPARATION TIME 15 MINUTES **SERVES** 4

300g sliced smoked salmon
2 ruby red grapefruits (700g)
2 tablespoons olive oil
1 teaspoon dijon mustard
150g mizuna
1/3 cup (50g) roasted cashews,
   chopped coarsely
1/2 small red onion (50g), sliced thinly

1 Reserve four slices of salmon; cut remaining slices into thick pieces.
2 Segment grapefruits over large bowl; add oil, mustard, mizuna, nuts, onion and fish pieces, mix gently.
3 Divide salad among serving plates; top with reserved salmon slices.

per serving 19.1g total fat (3g saturated fat); 1229kJ (294 cal); 8.6g carbohydrate; 21.1g protein; 2.4g fibre

lamb and fetta salad with warm walnut dressing

PREPARATION TIME 15 MINUTES
COOKING TIME 10 MINUTES **SERVES** 4

1 tablespoon vegetable oil
600g lamb fillets
200g fetta, crumbled
250g witlof, trimmed, leaves separated
150g baby spinach leaves, trimmed

WARM WALNUT DRESSING
2 cloves garlic, crushed
1 teaspoon finely grated lemon rind
1/4 cup (60ml) olive oil
2 tablespoons cider vinegar
1/2 cup (55g) coarsely chopped
   roasted walnuts

1 Heat oil in large frying pan; cook lamb, uncovered, about 10 minutes. Cover; stand 5 minutes then slice thickly.
2 Make warm walnut dressing.
3 Combine lamb in medium bowl with cheese, witlof and spinach. Serve salad drizzled with dressing.
WARM WALNUT DRESSING Cook garlic, rind, oil and vinegar in small pan, stirring, until hot. Remove from heat; stir in nuts.

per serving 52.8g total fat (16.8g saturated fat); 2742kJ (656 cal); 1.2g carbohydrate; 43.8g protein; 3.2g fibre

We think salsa verde is just as good as pesto, and deserving of far more attention. It's not a spicy Mexican salsa, but Italian, with a zesty, herbaceous, lemony flavour. The herbs used in salsa verde can vary, but it always contains mint and parsley.

mixed tomatoes on cheesy polenta with dill salsa verde

PREPARATION TIME 25 MINUTES (PLUS REFRIGERATION TIME)
COOKING TIME 25 MINUTES **SERVES** 4

1 litre (4 cups) water
1 cup (170g) polenta
20g butter
1 cup (80g) finely grated parmesan
200g red grape tomatoes, halved
200g yellow grape tomatoes, halved

DILL SALSA VERDE
1/2 cup finely chopped fresh flat-leaf parsley
1/4 cup finely chopped fresh mint
1/4 cup finely chopped fresh dill
1/4 cup finely chopped fresh chives
1 tablespoon wholegrain mustard
2 tablespoons lemon juice
2 tablespoons drained capers, rinsed,
   chopped finely
1 clove garlic, crushed
1/3 cup (80ml) olive oil

1 Oil deep 19cm-square cake pan.
2 Place the water in large saucepan; bring to a boil. Gradually stir polenta into water; simmer, stirring, about 10 minutes or until polenta thickens, stir in butter and cheese. Spread polenta into pan; cool 10 minutes. Refrigerate about 1 hour or until firm.
3 Combine ingredients for dill salsa verde in small bowl.
4 Combine tomatoes in medium bowl with a little of the salsa.
5 Turn polenta onto board; trim edges. Cut polenta into four squares; cut squares into two triangles. Cook polenta, both sides, in heated oiled grill pan until browned.
6 Serve polenta with tomato mixture and remaining salsa.
per serving 29.9g total fat (9.5g saturated fat); 1902kJ (455 cal); 32.9g carbohydrate; 12.2g protein; 3.9g fibre

This robust salad can be made ahead with great success: the flavours of the dressing's fresh oregano and lemon will permeate the grilled vegetables and make them even more delicious.

char-grilled mediterranean vegetables in fresh oregano dressing

PREPARATION TIME 20 MINUTES
COOKING TIME 35 MINUTES **SERVES** 4

1 medium red capsicum (200g)
1 medium yellow capsicum (200g)
1 large red onion (300g),
   halved, cut into wedges
1 small kumara (250g),
   sliced thinly lengthways
2 baby eggplants (120g),
   sliced thinly lengthways
2 medium zucchini (240g),
   halved lengthways
340g jar artichoke hearts, drained, halved
100g seeded kalamata olives
1 small radicchio (150g),
   trimmed, leaves separated

FRESH OREGANO DRESSING
1/4 cup (60ml) olive oil
2 tablespoons red wine vinegar
2 tablespoons lemon juice
2 cloves garlic, crushed
1 tablespoon finely chopped
   fresh oregano leaves

1 Quarter capsicums, remove and discard seeds and membranes; cut capsicum into thick strips.
2 Combine ingredients for fresh oregano dressing in screw-top jar; shake well.
3 Cook capsicum, in batches, on heated oiled grill plate (or grill or barbecue) until browned and tender. Cook onion, kumara, eggplant, zucchini and artichoke, in batches, on grill plate until browned.
4 Combine char-grilled vegetables, olives and dressing in large bowl; toss gently. Serve with radicchio.
per serving 14.8g total fat (2g saturated fat); 1104kJ (264 cal); 22.8g carbohydrate; 6.4g protein; 7.6g fibre

spicy citrus prawn and tat soi salad

PREPARATION TIME 20 MINUTES (PLUS REFRIGERATION TIME)
COOKING TIME 10 MINUTES **SERVES** 4

1kg uncooked medium king prawns
1 teaspoon finely grated orange rind
2 tablespoons orange juice
1 tablespoon sambal oelek
2 lebanese cucumbers (260g)
2cm piece fresh ginger (10g), grated
2 tablespoons olive oil
1/4 cup (60ml) rice vinegar
2 tablespoons orange juice
2 teaspoons fish sauce
1 tablespoon grated palm sugar
2 tat soi (300g), trimmed
1/2 cup firmly packed fresh mint leaves

1 Shell and devein prawns, leaving tails intact. Combine prawns in medium bowl with rind, juice and half the sambal. Cover; refrigerate 30 minutes.
2 Using vegetable peeler, slice cucumber into ribbons.
3 Cook prawns in large frying pan, in batches, until just changed in colour.
4 Combine prawns in large bowl with cucumber, remaining sambal and remaining ingredients; toss gently.
per serving 1.1g total fat (0.2g saturated fat); 665kJ (159 cal); 7.9g carbohydrate; 27.2g protein; 2.9g fibre

TAT SOI IS ALSO KNOWN AS SPOON CABBAGE BECAUSE OF THE ROUND, HOLLOW SHAPE OF ITS PEPPERY LEAVES

Cajun spice mix, a blend of ground herbs and spices that can include basil, paprika, tarragon, fennel, thyme or cayenne, is available at most supermarkets and speciality spice shops.

cajun-spiced beef and garlicky bean salad

PREPARATION TIME 15 MINUTES
COOKING TIME 10 MINUTES **SERVES** 4

750g piece beef fillet
1 tablespoon cajun spice mix
420g can mixed beans, rinsed, drained
2 lebanese cucumbers (260g), halved
  lengthways, sliced thinly
4 small tomatoes (360g), cut into wedges
1 medium red onion (170g), sliced thinly
1 medium avocado (250g), sliced thickly
$1/2$ cup finely chopped fresh coriander

GARLIC VINAIGRETTE
$1/4$ cup (60ml) lemon juice
$1/4$ cup (60ml) olive oil
2 cloves garlic, crushed

1 Combine ingredients for garlic vinaigrette in small bowl.
2 Sprinkle beef both sides with spice mix; cook on heated oiled grill plate (or grill or barbecue). Cover; stand 5 minutes then slice thinly.
3 Combine remaining ingredients in large bowl with dressing; toss gently. Serve salad topped with beef.
per serving 35.3g total fat (8.8g saturated fat); 2445kJ (585 cal); 16.3g carbohydrate; 47.5g protein; 7.5 g fibre

salad of grilled vegetables, haloumi and rosemary chicken

PREPARATION TIME 15 MINUTES
COOKING TIME 35 MINUTES **SERVES** 4

2 tablespoons olive oil
1 tablespoon balsamic vinegar
2 cloves garlic, crushed
1 tablespoon coarsely chopped
  fresh rosemary
800g chicken thigh fillets
600g piece pumpkin, trimmed, sliced thinly
300g asparagus, trimmed
2 x 180g packets haloumi cheese
250g rocket, trimmed

ROSEMARY BALSAMIC DRESSING
2 tablespoons olive oil
1 tablespoon balsamic vinegar
1 tablespoon lemon juice
1 tablespoon coarsely chopped
  fresh rosemary leaves

1 Combine ingredients for rosemary balsamic dressing in screw-top jar; shake well.
2 Combine oil, vinegar, garlic, rosemary and chicken in medium bowl. Cook chicken on heated oiled grill plate (or grill or barbecue); cover.
3 Cook pumpkin and asparagus, in batches, on grill plate until tender. Transfer to large bowl; cover.
4 Slice cheese thickly; cook on cleaned grill plate until browned both sides.
5 Slice chicken thickly. Combine with cheese, rocket and dressing in bowl with pumpkin and asparagus; toss gently.
per serving 49.1g total fat (17.2g saturated fat); 3106kJ (743 cal); 12.2g carbohydrate; 62.6g protein; 3.8g fibre

five-spice pork and nashi in chilli plum dressing

PREPARATION TIME 10 MINUTES (PLUS REFRIGERATION TIME)
COOKING TIME 20 MINUTES **SERVES** 4

600g pork fillets, trimmed
2 teaspoons vegetable oil
1 teaspoon five-spice powder
300g mizuna
2 green onions, sliced thinly
2 medium nashi (400g), sliced thinly

CHILLI PLUM DRESSING
¼ cup (60ml) plum sauce
1 tablespoon water
1 tablespoon lemon juice
1 fresh long red chilli, sliced thinly

1 Combine pork, oil and five-spice in large bowl; refrigerate 3 hours or overnight.

2 Combine ingredients for chilli plum dressing in screw-top jar; shake well.

3 Cook pork on heated oiled grill plate (or grill or barbecue) about 20 minutes. Cover; stand 10 minutes then slice thickly.

4 Combine mizuna, onion and nashi in large bowl with two-thirds of the dressing. Serve salad topped with pork, drizzled with remaining dressing.

per serving 14.8g total fat (4.3g saturated fat); 1522kJ (364 cal); 22.5g carbohydrate; 33.3g protein; 3.1g fibre

Wild rice blend is a pre-made mixture of white long-grain and wild rice. The latter, the seed of a North American aquatic grass, has a distinctively nutty flavour and crunchy, resilient texture.

greek-style wild rice salad with lemon and garlic yogurt

PREPARATION TIME 15 MINUTES
COOKING TIME 20 MINUTES **SERVES** 6

2 cups (400g) wild rice blend
1 medium red capsicum (200g)
1 medium brown onion (150g), quartered
250g cherry tomatoes
350g broccolini, halved crossways
1/2 cup (80g) roasted pine nuts
1 cup coarsely chopped fresh
   flat-leaf parsley
2 tablespoons lemon juice

LEMON AND GARLIC YOGURT
2 cloves garlic, crushed
300g yogurt
1/4 cup (60ml) lemon juice

1 Combine ingredients for lemon and garlic yogurt in small bowl.
2 Cook rice in large saucepan of boiling water, uncovered, until tender; drain. Place in large serving bowl.
3 Quarter capsicum; discard seeds and membranes. Cook capsicum, onion and tomatoes on heated, oiled grill plate (or grill or barbecue) until tender. Chop capsicum and onion coarsely.
4 Boil, steam or microwave broccolini until tender.
5 Combine capsicum, onion, tomatoes, nuts, parsley and juice with rice. Serve salad topped with broccolini then yogurt.
per serving 11.6g total fat (1.7g saturated fat); 1007kJ (241 cal); 20.2g carbohydrate; 10.9g protein; 6.3g fibre

fattoush with harissa-rubbed lamb

PREPARATION TIME 30 MINUTES (PLUS REFRIGERATION TIME)
COOKING TIME 15 MINUTES **SERVES** 4

600g lamb backstraps
$1/4$ cup (75g) harissa
3 pocket pittas (255g)
$1/4$ cup (60ml) olive oil
3 medium tomatoes (450g), cut into wedges
1 large green capsicum (350g),
  sliced thickly
2 lebanese cucumbers (260g), halved,
  sliced thinly
$1/2$ cup coarsely chopped fresh mint
1 cup firmly packed fresh
  flat-leaf parsley leaves
$1/4$ cup (60ml) lemon juice
1 clove garlic, crushed

1 Combine lamb and harissa in medium bowl; rub harissa into lamb. Refrigerate 1 hour.
2 Preheat grill.
3 Heat 1 tablespoon of the oil in large frying pan; cook lamb. Cover; stand 5 minutes then slice thickly.
4 Split pittas in half; grill both sides until browned lightly.
5 Combine remaining ingredients in large bowl; break pitta into pieces over salad. Serve fattoush topped with lamb.
per serving 28.9g total fat (8.2g saturated fat); 2416kJ (578 cal); 36.7g carbohydrate; 39.6g protein; 6.4g fibre

chilli, lime and ginger barbecued octopus salad

PREPARATION TIME 25 MINUTES (PLUS REFRIGERATION TIME)
COOKING TIME 10 MINUTES **SERVES** 4

$1/4$ cup (60ml) olive oil
1 tablespoon finely grated lime rind
2 tablespoons lime juice
2 cloves garlic, crushed
3 fresh small red thai chillies, chopped finely
1kg cleaned baby octopus, halved lengthways
150g mizuna
100g snow peas, trimmed, halved
227g can water chestnuts, drained,
  rinsed, sliced thinly
1 medium red capsicum (200g), sliced thinly
$1 1/4$ cups (100g) bean sprouts
1 cup loosely packed fresh coriander leaves
1 fresh long red chilli, sliced thinly

SWEET LIME AND GINGER DRESSING
3cm piece fresh ginger (15g), grated
$1/4$ cup (60ml) peanut oil
2 tablespoons lime juice
1 tablespoon white wine vinegar
2 teaspoons white sugar

1 Combine oil, rind, juice, garlic, chilli and octopus in large bowl. Cover; refrigerate 3 hours or overnight.
2 Combine ingredients for sweet lime and ginger dressing in screw-top jar; shake well.
3 Cook octopus on heated oiled grill plate (or grill or barbecue) about 10 minutes.
4 Combine mizuna, peas, chestnuts, capsicum, sprouts and coriander in large bowl with dressing. Sprinkle salad with sliced chill; serve salad accompanied with octopus.
per serving 29.7g total fat (4.4g saturated fat); 2061kJ (493 cal); 10.1g carbohydrate; 44.5g protein; 4.3g fibre

grilled lamb and
lebanese chickpea salad

PREPARATION TIME 15 MINUTES (PLUS REFRIGERATION TIME)
COOKING TIME 10 MINUTES **SERVES** 4

3 cloves garlic, crushed
$^1/_4$ cup (60ml) lemon juice
1 tablespoon olive oil
2 teaspoons ground cumin
750g lamb backstraps
2 tablespoons lemon juice, extra
2 tablespoons olive oil, extra
800g can chickpeas, rinsed, drained
3 medium egg tomatoes (225g),
  cut into wedges
1 lebanese cucumber (130g), halved
  lengthways, sliced thinly
1 medium red onion (170g), sliced thinly
$^1/_2$ cup coarsely chopped fresh mint
$^1/_2$ cup coarsely chopped fresh
  flat-leaf parsley

1 Combine garlic, juice, oil and cumin in large bowl with lamb. Refrigerate 3 hours or overnight.
2 Drain lamb; reserve marinade. Cook lamb on heated, oiled grill plate (or grill or barbecue), brushing occasionally with marinade. Cover; stand 5 minutes then slice thinly.
3 Whisk extra juice and extra oil in large bowl, add remaining ingredients; toss gently to combine. Serve salad topped with lamb.

per serving 33.2g total fat (9.8g saturated fat); 2537kJ (607 cal); 23.3g carbohydrate; 49.5g protein; 9.1g fibre

Crème fraîche, a fermented cream having a slightly tangy, nutty flavour and velvety texture, can be used in both sweet and savoury dishes, in much the same way as sour cream.

oven-roasted beef fillet and beetroot with horseradish crème fraîche

PREPARATION TIME 10 MINUTES
COOKING TIME 35 MINUTES (PLUS STANDING TIME) **SERVES** 4

500g piece beef eye fillet, trimmed
2 tablespoons wholegrain mustard
1 tablespoon horseradish cream
2 tablespoons olive oil
1kg baby beetroots, trimmed
150g baby rocket leaves
2 lebanese cucumbers (260g), sliced thinly
1 cup loosely packed fresh
   flat-leaf parsley leaves

PARMESAN CROUTONS
1 small french bread stick (150g)
1 tablespoon olive oil
1/2 cup (40g) finely grated parmesan

HORSERADISH CRÈME FRAÎCHE
1/4 cup (60g) crème fraîche
2 tablespoons horseradish cream
1 tablespoon lemon juice

1 Preheat oven to hot (220°C/200°C fan-forced).
2 Tie beef with kitchen string at 3cm intervals. Combine mustard, horseradish and oil in small jug; brush beef all over with mixture.
3 Place beef in medium oiled baking dish with beetroots; roast, uncovered, 10 minutes.
4 Reduce heat to moderately hot (200°C/180°C fan-forced); roast about 20 minutes or until beef and beetroots are cooked. Cover beef; stand 15 minutes then slice thinly. Peel and halve beetroots.
5 Make parmesan croutons. Combine ingredients for horseradish crème fraîche in small bowl.
6 Combine rocket, cucumber, parsley and beetroot in large bowl. Serve salad topped with croutons and beef, drizzled with crème fraîche.
PARMESAN CROUTONS Slice bread thinly; brush slices with oil, place on oven tray. Brown, in oven, towards end of beef cooking time; sprinkle with cheese, return to oven until cheese melts.
per serving 33.8g total fat (12.2g saturated fat); 2704kJ (647 cal); 40.7g carbohydrate; 40.2g protein; 10.5g fibre

crunchy cabbage, brazil nut and smoked chicken salad

PREPARATION TIME 20 MINUTES **SERVES** 4

800g smoked chicken breast fillets,
  sliced thinly
6 cups (480g) finely shredded wombok
1 medium red capsicum (200g),
  chopped coarsely
10 trimmed red radishes (150g), sliced thinly
4 green onions, sliced thinly
1/4 cup coarsely chopped fresh coriander
1/4 cup coarsely chopped fresh
  flat-leaf parsley
1/2 cup (80g) roasted brazil nuts,
  chopped coarsely

CHILLI LIME DRESSING
1/4 cup (60ml) lime juice
1 fresh long red chilli, chopped finely
1 tablespoon grated palm sugar
2 tablespoons fish sauce
2 teaspoons sesame oil

1   Combine ingredients for chilli lime dressing in screw-top jar; shake well.
2   Combine salad ingredients in large bowl with dressing.

per serving 30.2g total fat (7.3g saturated fat); 2240kJ (536 cal); 8.3g carbohydrate; 55.6g protein; 4.8g fibre

pasta salad with fried sprouts, bocconcini and almonds

PREPARATION TIME 20 MINUTES
COOKING TIME 15 MINUTES **SERVES** 6

500g rigatoni
1 tablespoon olive oil
300g brussels sprouts, trimmed, shredded
1/2 cup coarsely chopped fresh
   flat-leaf parsley
1 tablespoon drained capers, rinsed
200g bocconcini, sliced thickly
1/2 cup (80g) roasted almonds,
   chopped coarsely

RED WINE VINAIGRETTE
1/3 cup (80ml) lemon juice
1/3 cup (80ml) red wine vinegar
1/4 cup (60ml) olive oil
1 teaspoon white sugar
2 cloves garlic, crushed

1 Combine ingredients for red wine vinaigrette in screw-top jar; shake well.
2 Cook pasta in large saucepan of boiling water, uncovered, until just tender; drain. Place in large serving bowl.
3 Heat oil in same pan; stir-fry sprouts about 1 minute or until just warm.
4 Combine sprouts and remaining ingredients with pasta and vinaigrette; mix gently.
per serving 25.7g total fat (5.7g saturated fat); 2358kJ (564 cal); 60g carbohydrate; 19.9g protein; 6.2g fibre

asian pork and apple salad

PREPARATION TIME 20 MINUTES (PLUS REFRIGERATION TIME)
COOKING TIME 20 MINUTES **SERVES** 4

1/3 cup (80ml) hoisin sauce
1 tablespoon fish sauce
1 tablespoon light soy sauce
2 tablespoons rice vinegar
1/4 cup (90g) honey
1/2 teaspoon five-spice powder
2 cloves garlic, crushed
2cm piece fresh ginger (10g), grated
750g pork fillets, halved
1 tablespoon water
1/2 medium iceberg lettuce, chopped coarsely
50g bean sprouts
1 small red onion (100g), sliced thinly
1 medium green apple (150g), unpeeled,
   sliced thinly
1/3 cup firmly packed fresh mint leaves

1 Combine sauces, vinegar, honey, five-spice, garlic and ginger in medium jug.
2 Combine 1/2 cup (125ml) of the sauce mixture in medium bowl with pork. Cover; refrigerate 3 hours or overnight.
3 Stir the water into remaining sauce mixture; refrigerate.
4 Drain pork; reserve marinade. Cook pork on heated oiled grill plate (or grill or barbecue), brushing occasionally with marinade. Cover; stand 10 minutes then slice thickly.
5 Combine remaining ingredients in medium bowl. Top salad with pork; serve with reserved sauce.
per serving 16.4g total fat (5.3g saturated fat); 1923kJ (460 cal); 32.4g carbohydrate; 42.6g protein; 5.4g fibre

SIDES ADD CRISP FRESHNESS AND CONTRAST TO ANY MAIN COURSE, WHETHER IT'S A CREAMY SOUP OR THE SUNDAY ROAST

Pepitas, dried pumpkin seeds, are available hulled or unhulled, raw or roasted. Most people here usually eat them as a snack or in a homemade muesli, but in many other countries they are commonly ground into meal for use as a sauce thickener. Like nuts, pepitas go rancid easily, so it's best if they're kept, stored in an airtight container, in the refrigerator.

pepita and oak leaf lettuce salad with cranberry dressing

PREPARATION TIME 10 MINUTES **SERVES** 6

¹/₃ cup (65g) roasted pepitas
1 green oak leaf lettuce, leaves separated
1 small red onion (100g), sliced thinly

CRANBERRY DRESSING
2 tablespoons olive oil
2 tablespoons red wine vinegar
2 tablespoons cranberry sauce

1 Combine ingredients for cranberry dressing in screw-top jar; shake well.
2 Combine salad ingredients in medium bowl with dressing; toss gently.
per serving 9.8g total fat (0.9g saturated fat); 464kJ (111 cal); 4.4g carbohydrate; 0.7g protein; 2g fibre

italian-style bean salad with mozzarella, sun-dried tomato and olives

PREPARATION TIME 15 MINUTES
COOKING TIME 5 MINUTES **SERVES** 4

200g green beans, trimmed,
  halved crossways
2 x 420g cans four-bean mix, rinsed, drained
2 teaspoons finely chopped fresh thyme
2 teaspoons finely chopped fresh oregano
$^1/_3$ cup coarsely chopped fresh
  flat-leaf parsley
100g mozzarella, sliced thickly
$^3/_4$cup (110g) drained sun-dried
  tomatoes, sliced thinly
1 medium brown onion (150g), sliced thinly
1 cup (120g) seeded black olives

ITALIAN DRESSING
1 clove garlic, crushed
2 tablespoons olive oil
2 tablespoons lemon juice

1   Combine ingredients for italian dressing in screw-top jar; shake well.

2   Boil, steam or microwave green beans until tender; drain. Rinse under cold water; drain.

3   Combine green beans and four-bean mix in medium bowl with remaining ingredients and dressing; toss gently.

per serving 16.6g total fat (5.1g saturated fat); 1438kJ (344 cal); 28g carbohydrate; 15.6g protein; 10.5g fibre

Celeriac makes up in flavour what it lacks in looks. A knobbly brown tuber with crisp white flesh, it tastes like a sharper version of its near relative celery. It can be eaten raw, as here, in a delightfully crunchy salad, or cooked and mashed with butter, like potatoes.

celeriac remoulade

PREPARATION TIME 10 MINUTES **SERVES** 4

^{1}/$_3$ cup (100g) mayonnaise
1 clove garlic, crushed
^{1}/$_3$ cup (80g) sour cream
2 tablespoons lemon juice
2 teaspoons dijon mustard
650g celeriac, trimmed, grated coarsely
^{1}/$_2$ cup coarsely chopped fresh
  flat-leaf parsley

1 Combine mayonnaise in medium bowl with garlic, sour cream, juice and mustard.
2 Add celeriac and parsley; mix gently.
per serving 16.3g total fat (6.2g saturated fat); 920kJ (220 cal); 12.3g carbohydrate; 3.1g protein; 6.4g fibre

oak leaf and mixed herb salad with dijon vinaigrette

PREPARATION TIME 10 MINUTES **SERVES** 6

1 green oak leaf lettuce, leaves separated
^{1}/$_4$ cup coarsely chopped fresh chives
^{1}/$_2$ cup firmly packed fresh flat-leaf
  parsley leaves
^{1}/$_2$ cup firmly packed fresh chervil leaves

DIJON VINAIGRETTE
2 tablespoons olive oil
2 tablespoons white wine vinegar
1 tablespoon dijon mustard
2 teaspoons white sugar

1 Combine ingredients for dijon vinaigrette in screw-top jar; shake well.
2 Combine salad ingredients in medium bowl with dressing; toss gently.
per serving 6.2g total fat (0.9g saturated fat); 288kJ (69 cal); 2g carbohydrate; 0.7g protein; 1.1g fibre

barbecued potato salad with artichoke hearts in creamy mustard dressing

PREPARATION TIME 10 MINUTES
COOKING TIME 15 MINUTES **SERVES** 4

1kg kipfler potatoes, halved lengthways
1 tablespoon olive oil
8 cloves garlic, halved
340g jar artichoke hearts, drained, quartered
1 cup firmly packed fresh flat-leaf
   parsley leaves

CREAMY MUSTARD DRESSING
1 tablespoon balsamic vinegar
1 tablespoon american mustard
1/2 cup (125ml) cream

1 Combine ingredients for creamy mustard dressing in screw-top jar; shake well.
2 Boil, steam or microwave potato until tender; drain. Combine potato with oil in medium bowl.
3 Cook potato, garlic and artichoke, in batches, on heated oiled grill plate (or grill or barbecue) until potato is browned.
4 Return vegetables to same bowl with parsley; mix gently. Serve salad drizzled with dressing.
per serving 18.8g total fat (9.6g saturated fat); 1522kJ (364 cal); 35.4g carbohydrate; 8.6g protein; 8.5g fibre

KIPFLERS, ELONGATED FINGER-SHAPED POTATOES, HAVE A NUTTY FLAVOUR AND ARE GOOD ROASTED OR IN SALADS

green bean and tomato salad
with mustard hazelnut dressing

PREPARATION TIME 10 MINUTES
COOKING TIME 10 MINUTES **SERVES** 4

200g green beans, trimmed
250g cherry tomatoes, halved

MUSTARD HAZELNUT DRESSING
1/2 cup (70g) roasted hazelnuts,
  skinned, chopped coarsely
2 tablespoons hazelnut oil
2 tablespoons cider vinegar
1 teaspoon wholegrain mustard

1 Combine ingredients for mustard hazelnut dressing in screw-top jar; shake well.
2 Boil, steam or microwave beans until tender; drain. Rinse under cold water; drain.
3 Combine beans, tomato and dressing in medium bowl; toss gently.
per serving 20.2g total fat (1.8g saturated fat); 920kJ (220 cal); 3.6g carbohydrate; 4.2g protein; 4.3g fibre

cos, avocado and tomato salad

PREPARATION TIME 15 MINUTES **SERVES** 4

1 baby cos lettuce
3 medium tomatoes (450g), chopped finely
2 medium avocados (500g), chopped finely
1 lebanese cucumber (130g), chopped finely
1 small red onion (100g), chopped finely
¼ cup coarsely chopped fresh coriander
¼ cup (60ml) lime juice
2 cloves garlic, crushed

1 Separate lettuce leaves. Reserve several of the larger leaves; shred remaining leaves coarsely.
2 Combine shredded lettuce in medium bowl with remaining ingredients. Serve salad divided among reserved leaves.
per serving 20.2g total fat (4.3g saturated fat); 970kJ (232 cal); 5.8g carbohydrate; 4.3g protein; 4.8g fibre

moroccan orange and radish salad

PREPARATION TIME 20 MINUTES (PLUS REFRIGERATION TIME)
SERVES 4

10 trimmed medium red radishes (150g), sliced thinly
4 large oranges (1.2kg), segmented
1 small red onion (100g), sliced thinly
2 tablespoons coarsely chopped fresh flat-leaf parsley
2 tablespoons coarsely chopped fresh coriander
¼ cup (60ml) orange juice

1 Assemble radish, orange and onion on serving platter; sprinkle with parsley and coriander, drizzle with juice.
2 Cover salad; refrigerate 1 hour before serving.
per serving 0.3g total fat (0g saturated fat); 447kJ (107 cal); 20.1g carbohydrate; 3g protein; 5.2g fibre

broad bean, char-grilled corn and capsicum salad

PREPARATION TIME 15 MINUTES
COOKING TIME 15 MINUTES **SERVES** 4

1 medium red capsicum (200g)
1 fresh long red chilli
300g frozen broad beans
2 trimmed corn cobs (500g)
1 cup loosely packed fresh
  flat-leaf parsley leaves

GARLIC DRESSING
1 clove garlic, crushed
1 teaspoon caster sugar
$1/4$ cup (60ml) white wine vinegar
1 tablespoon olive oil

1 Quarter capsicum; discard seeds and membranes. Halve chilli lengthways. Cook capsicum and chilli on heated, oiled grill plate (or grill or barbecue), skin-side down, until skin blackens. Chop chilli finely. Cover capsicum for 5 minutes; peel away skin, chop coarsely.

2 Boil, steam or microwave beans until tender; drain. Rinse under cold water; drain. Peel away grey outer shells.

3 Combine ingredients for garlic dressing in screw-top jar; shake well.

4 Cook corn on grill plate until tender. Cut into thick slices; combine in large bowl with capsicum, beans, chilli, parsley and dressing; mix gently.

per serving 6g total fat (0.7g saturated fat); 886kJ (2121 cal); 24.1g carbohydrate; 8.9g protein; 11.7g fibre

pear, walnut and fetta salad with walnut dressing

PREPARATION TIME 20 MINUTES **SERVES** 4

1 butter lettuce
1 medium pear (230g), cored
1/3 cup (35g) roasted walnuts,
  chopped coarsely
40g snow pea sprouts, trimmed
50g fetta, crumbled
35g shaved parmesan

WALNUT DRESSING
1 tablespoon walnut oil
2 teaspoons wholegrain mustard
2 tablespoons white wine vinegar
1 tablespoon finely chopped fresh chives

1 Combine ingredients for walnut dressing in screw-top jar; shake well.
2 Separate lettuce leaves; tear leaves roughly.
3 Slice unpeeled pear into thin wedges.
4 Combine lettuce, pear and dressing in large bowl with remaining ingredients; toss gently.

per serving 16.6g total fat (5g saturated fat); 957kJ (229 cal); 10.4g carbohydrate; 8.4g protein; 3.3g fibre

USE ANY PEAR YOU LIKE IN THIS SALAD, AS LONG AS IT'S FIRM, CRUNCHY AND HOLDS ITS SHAPE WHEN CUT

Don't chop the mint until just before making this salad – it tends to blacken and go limp after it's been cut. We used a fairly bland fetta here so that its flavour didn't overpower the melon.

watermelon, mint and fetta salad

PREPARATION TIME 10 MINUTES **SERVES** 4

2 teaspoons white sugar
$^1/_4$ cup (60ml) lime juice
$^1/_2$ cup (100g) crumbled fetta
$^1/_2$ small red onion (50g), sliced thinly
$^1/_2$ cup coarsely chopped fresh mint
850g seedless watermelon, cut into wedges

1 Dissolve sugar in small jug with juice.
2 Combine juice in large bowl with cheese, onion and mint; spoon over watermelon.
per serving 6.2g total fat (3.8g saturated fat); 506kJ (121 cal); 10.1g carbohydrate; 5.4g protein; 1.5g fibre

rocket, parmesan and semi-dried tomato salad

PREPARATION TIME 10 MINUTES **SERVES** 4

1 tablespoon balsamic vinegar
1 tablespoon olive oil
100g baby rocket leaves
2 tablespoons roasted pine nuts
40g drained semi-dried tomatoes, chopped coarsely
$^1/_3$ cup (25g) flaked parmesan

1 Combine ingredients in large bowl; toss gently.
per serving 12.3g total fat (2.3g saturated fat); 635kJ (152 cal); 4.4g carbohydrate; 5.1g protein; 2.2g fibre

green and yellow split pea salad with wholegrain mustard dressing

PREPARATION TIME 10 MINUTES (PLUS STANDING TIME)
COOKING TIME 20 MINUTES **SERVES** 6

1/2 cup (100g) yellow split peas
1/2 cup (100g) green split peas
4 green onions, sliced thinly
250g cherry tomatoes, halved
1/2 cup coarsely chopped fresh
   flat-leaf parsley

WHOLEGRAIN MUSTARD DRESSING
1/4 cup (60ml) lemon juice
1/4 cup (60ml) olive oil
1 tablespoon wholegrain mustard
2 cloves garlic, crushed

1   Place peas in medium bowl, cover with cold water; stand overnight, drain. Rinse under cold water; drain.
2   Place peas in medium saucepan, cover with boiling water. Simmer, covered, about 10 minutes or until peas are tender; rinse under cold water, drain.
3   Whisk ingredients for wholegrain mustard dressing in small bowl.
4   Combine peas in large bowl with remaining ingredients and dressing; mix gently.
per serving 9.9g total fat (1.4g saturated fat); 836kJ (200 cal); 17.3g carbohydrate; 8.3g protein; 4.7g fibre

ALL DRIED LEGUMES WILL COOK FASTER IF COVERED WITH COLD WATER AND LEFT TO SOAK OVERNIGHT

three-bean salad with lemon chilli breadcrumbs

PREPARATION TIME 5 MINUTES
COOKING TIME 20 MINUTES **SERVES** 6

150g green beans, trimmed
150g yellow beans, trimmed
300g frozen broad beans
2 tablespoons olive oil
2 tablespoons lemon juice

LEMON CHILLI BREADCRUMBS
25g butter
1 tablespoon finely grated lemon rind
$1/3$ cup (25g) stale breadcrumbs
$1/4$ teaspoon chilli powder

1 Make lemon chilli breadcrumbs.

2 Boil, steam or microwave green, yellow and broad beans, separately, until tender; drain. Rinse under cold water; drain. Peel away grey outer shells from broad beans.

3 Combine all beans in medium bowl with oil and juice; sprinkle with breadcrumbs.

LEMON CHILLI BREADCRUMBS Melt butter in small frying pan; cook remaining ingredients over low heat, stirring, until crumbs are browned.

per serving 10g total fat (3.2g saturated fat); 594kJ (142 cal); 5.3g carbohydrate; 5.2g protein; 4.8g fibre

THESE DRESSINGS ARE SO EASY TO MAKE THAT YOU'LL NEVER USE A BOTTLED ONE AGAIN. EACH OF THESE RECIPES MAKES 1 CUP

rocket and garlic mayonnaise

PREPARATION TIME 5 MINUTES **SERVES** 4

1 cup (300g) mayonnaise
50g baby rocket leaves, trimmed
1 clove garlic, crushed
1 teaspoon finely grated lemon rind

1 Blend or process ingredients until smooth.
per serving 24.1g total fat (2.9g saturated fat); 1162kJ (278 cal); 14.7g carbohydrate; 1g protein; 0.8g fibre

creamy oregano and caper

PREPARATION TIME 10 MINUTES **SERVES** 4

2 hard-boiled eggs, quartered
1 tablespoon drained capers, rinsed
2 tablespoons white wine vinegar
2 tablespoons coarsely chopped
   fresh oregano
1 clove garlic, quartered
1/3 cup (80ml) olive oil

1 Blend or process egg, capers, vinegar, oregano and garlic until smooth. With motor operating, add oil in a thin, steady stream until dressing thickens.
per serving 20.9g total fat (3.4g saturated fat); 836kJ (200 cal); 0.5g carbohydrate; 3.4g protein; 0.2g fibre

green goddess

PREPARATION TIME 10 MINUTES **SERVES** 4

1 cup (300g) mayonnaise
2 anchovy fillets, drained, chopped finely
2 green onions, sliced thinly
2 teaspoons finely chopped
  fresh flat-leaf parsley
2 teaspoons finely chopped fresh chives
2 teaspoons finely chopped fresh tarragon
2 teaspoons cider vinegar

1 Combine ingredients in small bowl.

per serving 24.2g total fat (2.9g saturated fat); 1166kJ (279 cal); 14.6g carbohydrate; 1.2g protein; 0.6g fibre

thousand island

PREPARATION TIME 10 MINUTES **SERVES** 4

$1/2$ cup (150g) mayonnaise
$1^{1}/_{2}$ tablespoons tomato sauce
$1/2$ small white onion (40g), grated finely
8 pimiento-stuffed green olives,
  chopped finely
$1/2$ small red capsicum (75g), chopped finely

1 Combine ingredients in small bowl.

per serving 12.9g total fat (1.6g saturated fat); 681kJ (163 cal); 10.4g carbohydrate; 0.9g protein; 1.5g fibre

GLOSSARY

ARTICHOKE HEARTS tender centre of the globe artichoke; available fresh from the plant or preserved, canned, in brine.

BACON RASHERS also known as bacon slices; made from cured and smoked pork side.

BAY LEAVES aromatic leaves from the bay tree; used to flavour soups, stews and stocks.

BEANS
broad also known as fava, windsor and horse beans, these are available dried, fresh, canned and frozen. Fresh and frozen, they are best peeled twice (discard the outer long green pod and the grey-green tough inner shell).
green also called french or string beans.
sprouts also known as bean shoots; tender new growths of assorted beans and seeds germinated for consumption as sprouts.
yellow also known as wax, french, runner and (incorrectly) butter beans; basically a yellow-coloured fresh green bean.

BEETROOT also known as red beets or just beets; firm, round root vegetable.

BROCCOLINI a cross between broccoli and chinese kale; is milder and sweeter than traditional broccoli. Substitute gai lan or common broccoli.

BUK CHOY also known as bak choy, pak choi, chinese white cabbage or chinese chard; has a fresh, mild mustard taste.

BURGHUL also known as bulghur or bulgar wheat; hulled steamed wheat kernels that, once dried, are crushed into various size grains. Not the same as cracked wheat. Used in Middle-Eastern dishes such as kibbeh and tabbouleh; found in most supermarkets or health food stores.

BUTTERMILK sold in the dairy compartment in supermarkets. Originally the term given to the slightly sour liquid left after butter was churned from cream, today it is commercially made similarly to yogurt.

CAPERBERRIES fruit formed after the caper buds have flowered; caperberries are pickled, usually with stalks intact.

CAPERS the grey-green buds of a warm climate (usually Mediterranean) shrub; sold either dried and salted or pickled in a vinegar brine. Tiny young ones, called *baby capers*, are also available.

CAPSICUM also known as bell pepper or, simply, pepper. Seeds and membranes should be discarded before use.

CHEESE
bocconcini the term used for walnut-sized, baby mozzarella, a delicate, semi-soft, white cheese. Spoils rapidly so must be kept under refrigeration, in brine, for 1 or 2 days.
fetta a crumbly goat- or sheep-milk cheese with a sharp salty taste.
goat made from goat milk, has an earthy, strong taste; available in both soft and firm textures, in various shapes and sizes, sometimes rolled in ash or herbs.
haloumi a firm, cream-coloured sheep-milk cheese matured in brine. Somewhat like a minty, salty fetta in flavour; can be grilled or fried, briefly, without breaking down.
parmesan also known as parmigiano, grana or reggiano; a hard, grainy cow-milk cheese.
pecorino an Italian hard, white to pale yellow, flaky sheep-milk cheese.

CHERVIL also known as cicily; mildly fennel-flavoured herb with curly dark-green leaves.

CHICKPEAS also called garbanzos, hummus or channa; a sandy-coloured, irregularly round legume used extensively in Latin and Mediterranean cooking.

CHINESE BARBECUED DUCK traditionally cooked in special ovens, it has a sweet-sticky coating made from soy sauce, five-spice, sherry and hoisin sauce. Available from Asian food stores and specialty barbecue shops.

CHINESE BARBECUED PORK also called char siew. Traditionally cooked in special ovens, it has a sweet-sticky coating made from soy sauce, sherry, five-spice powder and hoisin sauce. Available from Asian food stores and specialty barbecue shops.

CHIVES related to the onion and leek; have a subtle onion flavour.

CHORIZO a sausage of Spanish origin, made of coarsely ground pork and highly seasoned with garlic, paprika and chilli.

CIABATTA in Italian, the word means slipper, which is the traditional shape of this popular crisp-crusted white bread.

CORIANDER also known as cilantro or chinese parsley; bright-green-leafed herb with a pungent flavour. Both the stems and roots of coriander are used in Thai cooking; wash well before chopping.

COUSCOUS a fine, grain-like cereal product from North Africa; made from semolina.

CRAISINS dried sweetened cranberries.

CRÈME FRAÎCHE mature fermented cream having a slightly tangy, nutty flavour and velvety texture.

EGG some of the recipes in this book call for raw or slightly cooked egg; exercise caution if there is a salmonella problem in your area.

EGGPLANT also known as aubergine; ranges in size from tiny to very large and in colour from pale green to deep purple.

FENNEL a crunchy green vegetable also known as finocchio or anise. The same name is given to its dried seeds, which have a strong licorice flavour.

FIVE-SPICE POWDER a fragrant mixture of ground cinnamon, cloves, star anise, sichuan pepper and fennel seeds. Also known as chinese five-spice.

FRIED NOODLES packaged deep-fried crispy wheat noodles; the crunchy base for dishes such as chow mein and sang choy bow.

GINGER also known as green or root ginger; the thick gnarled root of a tropical plant. Dried ground ginger is not a satisfactory substitute.

HARISSA a Moroccan paste used as a sauce or condiment; made from dried chillies, cumin, garlic, oil and caraway seeds. Available in supermarkets and Middle Eastern shops.

HORSERADISH
cream a prepared paste of grated horseradish, mustard seed, oil and sugar.
prepared unadulterated grated white horseradish in a vinegar brine.

KIPFLER POTATOES small, finger-shaped potato with a nutty flavour.

KITCHEN STRING made of a natural product, such as cotton or hemp, so it doesn't affect the flavour of the food it's tied around nor melts when heated.

KUMARA Polynesian name of orange-fleshed sweet potato often confused with yam.

LEAFY GREENS
coral a very curly, furled-leafed lettuce, comes in both light green and deep red varieties.
cos also known as romaine lettuce; the traditional Caesar salad lettuce.
curly endive also known as frisée; a green, curly-leafed vegetable.
iceberg a heavy, firm round lettuce with tightly packed leaves and crisp texture.
mesclun a salad mix of assorted young lettuce and other green leaves, including baby spinach, mizuna and curly endive.

mizuna Japanese in origin; a feathery green salad leaf with a sharp, slightly mustardy flavour. Found in most greengrocers.

oak leaf also known as feville de chenel; available in both red and green leaf varieties.

radicchio a member of the chicory family. Has dark burgundy leaves and a strong bitter flavour.

rocket also known as arugula, rugula and rucola; a peppery-tasting green leaf that can be used similarly to baby spinach leaves. *Baby rocket* leaves are smaller and less peppery.

LEBANESE CUCUMBER short, slender and thin-skinned; this variety is very popular due to its tiny seeds and flavoursome flesh.

LEMON GRASS a tall, clumping, lemon-smelling and tasting, sharp-edged grass; the white lower part of each stem is chopped and used in Asian cooking or for tea.

MANDARIN small, loose-skinned citrus fruit also known as tangerine. Segments in a light syrup are available canned.

MANGO tropical fruit originally from India and South-East Asia, now grown extensively here. Skin colour can range from green through yellow to deep red. Fragrant, deep-yellow flesh surrounds a large flat seed.

MAYONNAISE, WHOLE EGG high-quality commercial mayonnaise made with whole eggs and labelled as such. Must be refrigerated once opened.

MUSHROOMS

button small, cultivated white mushrooms having a delicate, subtle flavour.

flat large, flat mushrooms with a rich earthy flavour, ideal for filling and barbecuing. They are sometimes misnamed field mushrooms.

oyster also known as abalone; grey-white mushroom shaped like a fan. Prized for their smooth texture and subtle, oyster-like flavour.

shiitake when fresh, also known as chinese black or forest mushrooms; although cultivated, have the earthiness of wild mushrooms. Are often substituted for meat in Asian vegetarian dishes. When dried, known as donko or chinese mushrooms; rehydrate before use.

swiss brown also known as cremini or roman; light to dark brown mushrooms with full-bodied flavour. Button or cup mushrooms can be substituted, if desired.

MUSTARD

american also known as hot-dog mustard; bright yellow in colour and sweet, it's made from mustard seeds, sugar, spices and garlic.

dijon a pale brown, distinctively flavoured, fairly mild french mustard.

wholegrain also known as seeded mustard. A French-style coarse-grain mustard made from crushed mustard seeds and dijon-style french mustard.

NASHI a member of the pear family; resembles an apple with its pale-yellow-green, tennis-ball-sized appearance. More commonly known as the asian pear to much of the world. Its distinctive texture and mildly sweet taste make it perfect for use raw in salads, or as part of a cheese platter.

NUTS

pine nuts also known as pignoli; not, in fact, a nut, but a small, cream-coloured kernel from pine cones.

pistachio a pale green, delicately flavoured nut inside a hard off-white shell. *To peel*, soak shelled nuts in boiling water for about 5 minutes; drain then pat dry with absorbent paper. Rub skins with a dry cloth to peel.

OIL

hazelnut a mono-unsaturated oil extracted from crushed hazelnuts.

macadamia extracted from crushed macadamia nuts.

olive made from ripened olives. *Extra virgin* and *virgin* are the first and second press of the olives respectively, and are therefore considered the best, while *extra light* or *light* is diluted and refers to taste, not fat levels.

peanut pressed from ground peanuts; most commonly used oil in Asian cooking because of its high smoke point (capacity to handle high heat without burning).

sesame produced from roasted crushed white sesame seeds; a flavouring rather than a cooking medium.

vegetable any of a number of oils sourced from plants rather than animal fats.

ONIONS

green also known as scallion or, incorrectly, shallot; an immature onion picked before the bulb has formed, having a long, bright-green edible stalk.

red also known as spanish, red spanish or bermuda onion; a sweet-flavoured, large, purple-red onion that is particularly good eaten in raw salads.

shallot also called french shallots, golden shallots or eschalots; small, elongated, brown-skinned members of the onion family. Grows in tight clusters similar to garlic.

PANCETTA an Italian unsmoked bacon (cured pork belly). Is most often used, either sliced or chopped, as an ingredient to add its flavour to recipes rather than eaten on its own.

PAPRIKA from the Latin for pepper, the dried ground form of a specific variety of red capsicum of which there are a dozen different types; sold in sweet, smoked or hot flavours.

PARSLEY, FLAT-LEAF also known as continental or italian parsley.

PASTA

farfalle bow-tie shaped short pasta; also known as butterfly pasta.

macaroni a short, hollow pasta.

orecchiette small disc-shaped pasta, translates literally as "little ears".

penne translated literally as "quills"; ridged pasta cut on the diagonal into short lengths.

rigatoni a short, slightly curved tube pasta.

risoni small rice-shape pasta; very similar to another small pasta, orzo.

shell shell-shaped pasta ranging in size from tiny to very large.

spaghetti long, thin solid strands of pasta.

spiral corkscrew-shaped pasta.

PITTA also known as lebanese bread; a wheat-flour pocket bread sold in large, flat pieces that easily separate into two thin rounds. Also available in small thick pieces called *pocket pitta*.

POLENTA also known as cornmeal; a flour-like cereal made of dried corn (maize) and sold ground in several different textures; also the name of the dish made from it.

POMEGRANATE dark-red, leathery-skinned fresh fruit, about the size of an orange, filled with hundreds of seeds, each wrapped in an edible lucent-crimson pulp having a unique tangy sweet-sour flavour.

PRESERVED LEMON a North African specialty, the citrus is preserved, usually whole, in a mixture of salt and lemon juice. Found bottled in delicatessens and Middle Eastern food shops; once opened, store under refrigeration. Rinse well under cold water before using.

PROSCIUTTO an Italian ham, unsmoked, but salted, air-cured and aged. It is usually eaten uncooked.

SAMBAL OELEK (also ulek or olek) a salty paste made from ground chillies and vinegar; Indonesian in origin. Available from Asian food stores and most supermarkets.

SAUCES

barbecue a spicy, tomato-based sauce used to marinate, baste or as an accompaniment.

cranberry made of cranberries cooked in sugar syrup; its astringent flavour goes well with roast poultry and meats.

fish called naam pla or nuoc naam depending on where it is made. Made from pulverised salted fermented fish (most often anchovies); has a pungent smell and strong taste. There are many versions of varying intensity, so use according to your taste.

hoisin a thick, sweet and spicy chinese sauce made from salted fermented soy beans, onions and garlic; used as a marinade or baste, or to accent stir-fries and barbecued or roasted foods.

plum a thick, sweet and sour sauce made from plums, vinegar, sugar, chillies and spices.

soy also known as sieu, made from fermented soy beans. Several variations are available in most supermarkets and Asian food stores.

worcestershire a thin, dark-brown spicy sauce used as a seasoning for meat, gravies and cocktails and as a condiment.

SAVOY CABBAGE large, heavy head with crinkled dark-green outer leaves; a fairly mild tasting cabbage.

SCALLOPS a bivalve mollusc with fluted shell valve; we use scallops having the coral (roe) attached.

SESAME SEEDS black and white are the most common of this small oval seed, however, there are red and brown varieties also. A good source of calcium; used in cuisines the world over as an ingredient in cooking and as a condiment.

SHALLOT see onions.

SILVER BEET also known as swiss chard and incorrectly, spinach; has fleshy stalks and large, dark-green wrinkly leaves.

SNOW PEAS also called mange tout (eat all). *Snow pea sprouts*, the growing shoots of the plant, are sold by greengrocers.

SPINACH also known as english spinach and, incorrectly, silver beet. Tender green leaves are good uncooked in salads or added to soups, stir-fries and stews just before serving.

SPLIT PEAS also known as field peas; green or yellow pulse grown especially for drying, split in half along a centre seam. Used in soups, stews and, occasionally, spiced and cooked on their own.

SUGAR

brown an extremely soft, fine granulated sugar retaining molasses for its characteristic colour and flavour.

caster also known as superfine or finely granulated table sugar.

palm also known as jaggery or gula melaka; made from the sap of the sugar palm tree. Light- to dark-brown in colour and usually sold in rock-hard cakes. Substitute dark brown sugar if you can't find palm sugar.

white coarse, granulated table sugar, also known as crystal sugar.

SUGAR SNAP PEAS also known as honey snap peas; fresh small pea that can be eaten whole, pod and all, similarly to snow peas.

TAMARIND the tamarind tree produces clusters of hairy brown pods, each of which is filled with seeds and a viscous pulp that are dried and pressed into the blocks of tamarind found in Asian food shops. Gives a sweet-sour, slightly astringent taste to marinades, pastes, sauces and dressings.

TAMARIND CONCENTRATE (or paste) is the commercial result of the distillation of tamarind juice into a condensed, compacted paste.

TANDOORI PASTE consisting of garlic, ginger, tamarind, coriander, chilli and spices.

TAT SOI also known as spoon cabbage, rosette, pak choy or chinese flat cabbage; a member of the same family as buk choy with the same mild flavour. Its petal-like leaves give a wonderful look to a salad; available at most greengrocers.

THAI BASIL also known as horapa; is different from holy basil and sweet basil in both look and taste, having smaller leaves and purplish stems. It has a slight licorice or aniseed taste, and is one of the basic flavours that typify Thai cuisine.

TOFU

an off-white, custard-like product, also known as bean curd, made from the milk of crushed soy beans; comes fresh as soft or firm, and processed as fried or pressed dried sheets.

silken tofu refers to the method by which it is made, strained through silk, and can apply to both soft and firm tofu.

TOMATO

cherry also known as tiny tim or tom thumb tomatoes, small and round.

egg also called plum or roma, these are smallish, oval-shaped tomatoes.

semi-dried partially dried tomato pieces in olive oil; softer and juicier than sun-dried, these are not a preserve thus do not keep as long as sun-dried.

sun-dried we used sun-dried tomatoes packaged in oil, unless otherwise stated.

TURMERIC a rhizome related to galangal and ginger; must be grated or pounded to release its somewhat acrid aroma and pungent flavour. Fresh turmeric can be substituted with the more common dried powder (use 2 teaspoons of ground turmeric plus a teaspoon of sugar for every 20g of fresh turmeric called for in a recipe).

VIETNAMESE MINT not a mint at all, but a pungent and peppery narrow-leafed member of the buckwheat family. It is a common ingredient in Thai foods, particularly soups, salads and stir-fries.

VINEGAR

balsamic originally from Modena, Italy, there are now many balsamic vinegars on the market ranging in pungency and quality depending on how, and how long, they have been aged. Quality can be determined up to a point by price; use the most expensive sparingly.

cider made from fermented apples. Available from supermarkets and health food stores.

raspberry made from fresh raspberries steeped in a white wine vinegar.

WATER CHESTNUTS resemble the chestnut in appearance, hence the English name. They are small brown tubers with a crisp, white, nutty-tasting flesh. Their crunchy texture is best experienced fresh, however, canned water chestnuts are easier to find.

WATERCRESS one of the cress family, a large group of peppery greens used raw in salads, dips and sandwiches, or cooked in soups. Highly perishable, so must be used as soon as possible after purchase.

WILD RICE BLEND a packaged mixture of white long-grain and wild rice. The latter is the seed of a North American aquatic grass, with a distinctively nutty flavour.

WITLOF also known as chicory or belgian endive; a pale green to white vegetable that can be eaten raw or cooked.

WOMBOK also known as chinese cabbage; elongated with pale green crinkly leaves, it is most commonly used in South-East Asia.

ZUCCHINI also called courgette. A member of the squash family, having edible flowers.

CONVERSION CHART

MEASURES

One Australian metric measuring cup holds approximately 250ml; one Australian metric tablespoon holds 20ml; one Australian metric teaspoon holds 5ml.

The difference between one country's measuring cups and another's is within a two- or three-teaspoon variance, and will not affect your cooking results. North America, New Zealand and the United Kingdom use a 15ml tablespoon.

All cup and spoon measurements are level. The most accurate way of measuring dry ingredients is to weigh them. When measuring liquids, use a clear glass or plastic jug with metric markings.

We use large eggs with an average weight of 60g.

DRY MEASURES

METRIC	IMPERIAL
15g	$^1/_2$oz
30g	1oz
60g	2oz
90g	3oz
125g	4oz ($^1/_4$lb)
155g	5oz
185g	6oz
220g	7oz
250g	8oz ($^1/_2$lb)
280g	9oz
315g	10oz
345g	11oz
375g	12oz ($^3/_4$lb)
410g	13oz
440g	14oz
470g	15oz
500g	16oz (1lb)
750g	24oz (1$^1/_2$lb)
1kg	32oz (2lb)

LIQUID MEASURES

METRIC	IMPERIAL
30ml	1 fluid oz
60ml	2 fluid oz
100ml	3 fluid oz
125ml	4 fluid oz
150ml	5 fluid oz ($^1/_4$ pint/1 gill)
190ml	6 fluid oz
250ml	8 fluid oz
300ml	10 fluid oz ($^1/_2$ pint)
500ml	16 fluid oz
600ml	20 fluid oz (1 pint)
1000ml (1 litre)	1$^3/_4$ pints

LENGTH MEASURES

METRIC	IMPERIAL
3mm	$^1/_8$in
6mm	$^1/_4$in
1cm	$^1/_2$in
2cm	$^3/_4$in
2.5cm	1in
5cm	2in
6cm	2$^1/_2$in
8cm	3in
10cm	4in
13cm	5in
15cm	6in
18cm	7in
20cm	8in
23cm	9in
25cm	10in
28cm	11in
30cm	12in (1ft)

OVEN TEMPERATURES

These oven temperatures are only a guide for conventional ovens.
For fan-forced ovens, check the manufacturer's manual.

	°C (CELSIUS)	°F (FAHRENHEIT)	GAS MARK
Very slow	120	250	$^1/_2$
Slow	150	275-300	1-2
Moderately slow	160	325	3
Moderate	180	350-375	4-5
Moderately hot	200	400	6
Hot	220	425-450	7-8
Very hot	240	475	9

INDEX

A

artichoke hearts with potato salad in creamy
   mustard dressing, barbecued 95
asian pork and apple salad 87
asparagus and spinach with poached egg
   and pecorino 6
avocado, cos and tomato salad 99

B

barbecued octopus salad, chilli, lime
   and ginger 79
barbecued pork and crunchy noodle salad 25
barbecued potato salad with artichoke
   hearts in creamy mustard dressing 95
bean salad, garlicky, and cajun-spiced beef 72
bean salad, italian-style, with mozzarella,
   sun-dried tomato and olives 91
bean, green, and tomato salad with mustard
   hazelnut dressing 96
bean, three-, salad with lemon
   chilli breadcrumbs 108
beef fillet, oven-roasted, and beetroot with
   horseradish crème fraîche 83
beef, thai 43
beef, cajun-spiced, and garlicky bean salad 72
beetroot, roasted, and potato with paprika
   mayonnaise 10
black grape, chicken and wild rice salad
   with tarragon dressing 56
bocconcini, almonds and fried sprouts with
   pasta salad 87
breadcrumbs, lemon chilli 108
brie and pecans with shaved fennel and
   apple salad 17
broad bean, char-grilled corn and
   capsicum salad 100

C

cabbage, brazil nut and smoked chicken
   salad, crunchy 84
caesar 41
cajun-spiced beef and garlicky bean salad 72
caprese 47
carpaccio with shaved parmesan and
   basil salsa verde 22
celeriac remoulade 92
char-grilled mediterranean vegetables
   in fresh oregano dressing 68
char-grilled scallop and witlof salad with
   orange gremolata 33
cheese, goat, fig and prosciutto salad 29
cheesy polenta with salsa verde, mixed
   tomatoes on 67
chicken chow-mein salad with raspberry
   macadamia dressing, smoked 21

chicken, black grape and wild rice salad
   with tarragon dressing 56
chicken, salad of grilled vegetables,
   haloumi and rosemary 72
chicken, shredded, three-cabbage
   coleslaw with 55
chicken, smoked, crunchy cabbage and
   brazil nut salad 84
chicken, tandoori, spinach and mint salad
   with spiced yogurt 60
chilli-lime green salad with mango and
   crisp-fried duck 59
chilli, lime and ginger barbecued
   octopus salad 79
chilli, salt and pepper squid 30
chorizo and lentil salad, warm 13
chorizo, curly endive, orange and
   walnut salad 10
coleslaw 43
coleslaw, three-cabbage with
   shredded chicken 55
cos, avocado and tomato salad 99
couscous, moroccan, salad with
   preserved lemon dressing 48
creamy oregano and caper dressing 110
crisp-fried duck and mango with
   chilli-lime green salad 59
croutons, parmesan 83
crunchy cabbage, brazil nut and
   smoked chicken salad 84
crunchy snow pea, prawn and avocado
   salad with chive vinaigrette 59

D

dressings
   caesar 41
   chilli lime 84
   chilli plum 75
   chive vinaigrette 59
   cranberry 88
   creamy horseradish 18
   creamy mustard 95
   creamy oregano and caper 110
   dijon vinaigrette 92
   dill lemon 6
   fennel slaw 55
   fresh oregano 68
   garlic 100
   garlic vinaigrette 72
   green goddess 113
   honey cider 29
   horseradish crème fraîche 83
   italian 91
   lemon buttermilk 22
   lemon and garlic yogurt 76

   lime and ginger 52
   mayonnaise (paprika) 10
   mayonnaise (potato) 37
   mayonnaise (rocket and garlic) 110
   mayonnaise (waldorf) 47
   mint aïoli 14
   mustard hazelnut 96
   mustard vinaigrette 17
   palm sugar and lime 9
   preserved lemon 48
   raspberry macadamia 21
   red wine vinaigrette 87
   rosemary balsamic 72
   spiced yogurt 60
   sweet lime and ginger 79
   sweet-sour 25
   tarragon 56
   thousand island 113
   walnut 103
   walnut orange 10
   walnut, warm 64
   wholegrain mustard 107
duck, crisp-fried, and mango with chilli-lime
   green salad 59

E

egg, poached, and pecorino with asparagus
   and spinach 6
eggplant, fetta and semi-dried tomato salad 18

F

fattoush with harissa-rubbed lamb 79
fennel and apple salad with brie and
   pecans, shaved 17
fetta and lamb salad with warm
   walnut dressing 64
fetta, eggplant and semi-dried tomato salad 18
fetta, watermelon and mint salad 104
fig, goat cheese and prosciutto salad 29
five-spice pork and nashi in chilli
   plum dressing 75

G

goat cheese, fig and prosciutto salad 29
grapefruit, ruby red, smoked salmon
   and mizuna 64
greek 38
greek-style wild rice salad with lemon
   and garlic yogurt 76
green and yellow split pea salad with
   wholegrain mustard dressing 107
green bean and tomato salad with mustard
   hazelnut dressing 96
green goddess dressing 113
gremolata, orange 33
grilled lamb and lebanese chickpea salad 80